When the Perfect Comes

The real challenge to the imperfect Church

David W. Percy

Copyright © 2008 David W. Percy

ISBN: 978-1-60383-096-6

Published by:
Holy Fire Publishing
717 Old Trolley Road
Attn: Suite 116, Publishing Unit #116
Summerville, SC 29485

www.ChristianPublish.com

Printed in the United States of America and the United Kingdom

It was during the early 1980s, when I first looked at the question of whether gifts ceased or remained. My Pastor at that time wrote a book called, "Charismatics and the Word of God". At the time I wasn't agreeing or disagreeing with whether gifts ceased, but having read 1 Corinthians I was unconvinced that Paul's letter was written to be used as an argument either for charismatic continuation or conservative cessation.

I was blown away by what God was saying about the work of His Holy Spirit in the Church of the Lord Jesus Christ and the purpose of that work, which is, I believe, as relevant today as ever.

Putting finger to keyboard, back in the eighties, I wrote about a hundred and eighty pages which I eventually lost.

Recently, I have been persuaded to re-write. Thankfully, my brother in law, Martin Luff had an original draft of about forty pages which, I was amazed to discover, still excited me.

I am aware that what I have written will conflict with established views. My purpose is not to criticise, but to make known my own discovery in the Word of God.

I am grateful to Becky White, who has translated my ragged efforts into something which can be read.

David W Percy

Table of Contents

Chapter 1

The Promised Holy Spirit . . .

As a young Pastor, several years ago, I was privileged to be seated for a meal with a group of clerical gentry whose discussion was already under way when I arrived.

"It's dreadful," commented one, "Dancing in the aisles. I don't know what the Church is coming to."

"Awful," responded another. "I think it's high time this tomfoolery stopped and we got back to the preaching of the Word."

"Absolutely," joined in the third. "The preaching of the Word is sadly neglected these days."

Eventually, as I was the only person present at the table who had not spoken, eyes were focused on me and a response seemed called for.

"Being men of the Word," I asked, "What would you do if the Bible said 'Praise the Lord with dancing'?" Their response was rather flustered.

"I think this is your question John," said one, quickly passing the buck to one of his colleagues. John faced the question full on.

"I think I'd … er … er … duck the issue."

During the last four decades, we have witnessed in the Church of the Lord Jesus Christ, a major upheaval which centres around a renewed acceptance of the gifts and ministries of the Holy Spirit. Much of this change has been most obviously reflected in styles of worship, some of which are more expressive, incorporating raised hands, singing and praying in tongues, and, yes, dancing in the aisles. While it might feel easier to "duck the issue" as my colleague was tempted to do, it seems evident that this is simply not an adequate response. As Christians, and especially as Pastors and Ministers, we must face up to the questions that are being raised about the work of the Holy Spirit in individuals and in churches.

As with every change which has ever been wrought in the Church throughout its history, many have counted it as a much needed blessing, whilst others have resisted such change as modernistic curse. It seems strange to me that the reformation took place, causing the most radical and necessary change in the Church in order to bring about a renewal of Biblical precept and evangelical truth. It now appears that the evangelical tradition, which was the plaster cast of healing of a major fracture, has become our walking impediment, preventing the Church from flexing its healed limbs. Whilst Jesus does not change, the Church must seek to be constantly reviewed by the Word of God. We seek to interpret the Word of God, but should the Word be allowed to interpret us? There are many areas in need of change – our tradition does not have everything right. God has. It is therefore only the working of His righteousness, His Word, His Holy Spirit,

His power and love, that that will ever change us to be like His Son.

Opinion amongst Christians as to whether the power of the Holy Spirit is still available today is still divided, and many books have been written, and much preached and taught in our congregations in support of one view or the other. Both Charismatics (those who exercise the gifts and ministries of the Spirit today) and Cessationists (who believe that the work of the Holy Spirit is not for today) have cited one particular passage in support of their particular argument. 1 Corinthians 13 verses 8 to10 reads:

> "Where there are prophecies, they
> will cease; where there are tongues
> they will be stilled; where there is
> knowledge it will pass away.   For

11

we know in part and we prophesy in part, but when the perfect comes, that which is in part will disappear."

The question which is generally raised is this: If gifts cease when the perfect comes, then when is the perfect come?

Here I state clearly my own convictions, in order that any ambiguity may be dispelled:

I am convinced by the demonstrable Word of God. That His Holy Spirit, as poured out at Pentecost, with every power and gift of God, is still being poured out today as then, and may be received by men and women now in exactly the same way.

While my convictions are amply supported by my own experience, I am also convinced that they are fully supported by the Word of God, both in the fact of the continuance of the pouring out of the Spirit, and in the ways in which we can expect to see that outpouring manifested in our own churches.

Acts chapter 2 still stands as one such immutable part of the Word of God. Some have sought to dismiss Acts as being a transitional book. Such dismissal does not behove the Lord's servant. If Acts is merely transitional then such invalidation of Scripture on the grounds of temporality must be applied to the rest of the Bible. God's Word can never be invalidated in this way. "All scripture is God breathed and useful for teaching, rebuking, correcting and training in righteousness, so that the man of God may be thoroughly equipped for every good work."

In Acts 2 verse 33, Peter, speaking of the Lord Jesus Christ, says this:

> "Exalted to the right hand of God, He has received from the Father the promised Holy Spirit and has poured out what you now see and hear."

He goes on to say in verses 38 and 39:

> "And you will receive the gift of the Holy Spirit. The promise is for

you and your children and for all who are far off, for all whom the Lord our God will call."

Every contrary argument does not remove this Word of God. The promise of the same Holy Spirit, as seen and heard, is for you and your children, for those who are far off and all those who God will call. If we resist the Holy Spirit in Pentecost, we resist the call of God

So, let us look at some of the difficult arguments that arise when establishing whether the gifts and ministries of the Holy Spirit are still available for Christians today. When does the perfect come?

Chapter 2

Some theories . . .

The Perfect Canon of Scripture?

Some who believe that the work of the Spirit has
ceased, (Cessationists), have pointed to, "the
perfect", canon of Scripture as the place where,
"the perfect", arrived and thus brought an end
to gifts, which were only available for revelation
until such time as the Bible was completed. It is
held that we have in the Scripture the perfect
revelation, therefore tongues, prophecies and
knowledge are no longer needed.

There is, however, not even a hint of a
suggestion in the Word that this is so. It is
merely an idea which fits in with a pattern of

logical, but unscriptural argument. Firstly, there is no contextual place in 1 Corinthians 13 where, "The perfect", canon of Scripture' could fit. Secondly, nowhere in the Word is there even a suggestion that gifts were given for the revelation of Scripture, with a view to their end upon its completion. Thirdly, there appear to be hundreds in the New Testament who were operating in the gifts of the Holy Spirit which seem to have no relevance to the revelation of Scripture; healing is an example of this. Fourthly, it is probably true that there were no more than seven writers of the New Testament after the Gospels. Why then does God choose to give His Holy Spirit to so many in such diverse ways?

In Acts 2, the Bible tells us that the prophet Joel had spoken about this. His prophesy cannot be regarded as 'transient' even by those who seek to dismiss the Acts of the Apostles. In Acts 2, verse 17, the prophet is quoted by Peter as he addresses the wondering crowd: "I will pour out my Spirit on all flesh", not just Scripture writers. He says "your sons and daughters will prophesy." If this Holy Spirit is given only to write Scripture, where are the prophecies of the "daughters" written?

Whilst everyone would, I am certain, agree that the Word of God was revealed by the Holy Spirit, there is no place, Biblical, logical, theological or otherwise for a belief in the cessation of gifts on the basis that the canon of Scripture is now complete. We will see later that the Holy Spirit was and continues to be given for the building up of the Church, not only the writing of scripture.

The Apostolic Era?

There have also been some endeavours to link gifts with apostleship in such an inextricable way that the early apostles were the only true bearers of gifts in a form which was communicable to others. This of course would mean that gifts would cease at the end of the 'apostolic era'. This phrase, 'apostolic era', is not a Biblical phrase but is terminology used to describe the life period of the first apostles who were, according to some cessationists, also the last apostles, because it is claimed that the apostles were necessarily those who had seen the resurrected Lord Jesus Christ. This of course included Paul, who met the risen Jesus on the road to Damascus.

Again, there are a number of difficulties with this theory, not least of which is that the Bible does not support it. The difficulties begin with how we define an 'apostle'. Apostles were not primarily people who bore witness to the resurrection, but primarily men sent by God. 1 Corinthians 15 verses 6 to 8 tells us that, "Jesus, after appearing to Peter and the brothers, then appeared to more than five hundred of the brothers and then to the apostles." The five hundred did meet with the resurrected Jesus and yet they are not counted as apostles. It could easily be asserted that the first person to bear witness to the resurrection was Mary Magdalene, who is neither mentioned as an apostle, nor a writer of Scripture. The one did not of necessity follow the other, so it cannot be sensibly asserted that the term apostle should apply only to those who saw Jesus, and that only those who saw the risen Lord can be called apostles. The term 'apostle' has a much broader meaning than that.

Some have laid great store by the fact that Paul said in verse 8, "And last of all he appeared to me also," emphasising that Paul is the last apostle and therefore also the last bearer of the communicable gifts. Let us look again at the Biblical facts here. Paul did not say that he was the last bearer of the communicable gifts, or even the last apostle. He said that he was the last to see the risen Lord. As we have already discussed, the title 'apostle' and the fact that Paul saw the risen Lord Jesus are not necessarily linked. He then received the gift of the Holy Spirit at the hand of a very average disciple. In Acts 9 verse 10, Ananias is referred to as disciple, not a gift communicating apostle. In Acts 9 verse 17, this disciple, who saw a vision in the Holy Spirit, laid hands on Paul, and Paul received the Holy Spirit at his hand.

As though this were not enough, in Acts 10 verse 46, after Paul's conversion, Peter was preaching at Cornelius' house when the Holy Spirit fell on a Gentile congregation. Peter said, "They have received the Holy Spirit, just as we have." Peter didn't lay hands on them; he was preaching at the time. The Holy Spirit Himself poured out over them. Is it possible that Peter got it wrong and should not have taken their experience as evidence? I submit that what Peter saw, evidenced by speaking in tongues – something which he too found hard to believe – was that the Holy Spirit was being poured out on all, just as He had been on him. If they received the gift just as Peter did, was it not communicable? Why did God do another outpouring rather than allow Peter to lay his hands on them? In fact, since they were not apostles or writers of the New Testament, why give them the Holy Spirit at all?

The Greek word *apostolos* speaks of a delegate or member; one sent forth with orders. To be an apostle, then, is to be sent by God. In the case of Paul and some of those who had been with Jesus from the beginning and seen him risen from the dead, their apostleship was to take the totality of the good news to the Jews and, in Paul's case, to the Gentiles also. Whilst this apostleship was specific, an apostleship was not limited to the one message any more than a postman is limited to one letter. If we look at Mark's gospel, chapter 3 verse 14, Jesus refers to the "apostles, that they might be with Him and that He might send them out to preach and to have authority over demons." Jesus directly links apostleship with being sent out and having authority. At this time, Jesus had not died or risen and so these apostles bore no witness to the resurrection.

Luke's Gospel expands on this in chapter 9. In verse 1, Jesus gives authority and power to the twelve. (Presumably Judas Iscariot was counted as an apostle at this time although he certainly never saw Jesus risen and did not receive the Pentecostal Holy Spirit). Jesus sent out the apostles to preach, heal the sick and cast out demons. They were sent – apostles. They were given authority and a commission; this was their apostleship. Verse 10 says "When the apostles returned." They already were apostles. They didn't have to wait for the resurrection, because an apostle is one who is sent. In Luke chapter

10, the Lord appointed others and sent them in the same manner, thereby extending this apostleship beyond the twelve. He anoints and appoints whom He wills.

Therefore, an apostle is sent and an apostleship is the calling and message with which he is sent. The authority and empowering of the Holy Spirit are to equip the one who is sent for the fulfilment of that calling. Paul's own apostleship is described in Romans 1 verse 5, as being "to call people from among all the Gentiles, to the obedience which comes from faith." There is no mention of resurrection. His apostleship is linked to his call and his message. Therefore, those who respond to God's call and go out with His message today could also be called apostles.

In 2 Corinthians 12 verse 12, Paul shares with us that the marks of an apostle are signs and wonders and miracles. If apostles have not ceased, then it follows that neither have callings nor gifts. In Acts chapter 13, we read how Paul and Barnabas received an apostleship. In verse 1, Saul and Barnabas are prophets or teachers or both, but not apostles. In verse 2, the Holy Spirit asks for them to be set apart for the work to which he has called them. Of course, in Acts 11 verse 22, Barnabas had previously been sent from Jerusalem to Antioch (*exapostello*, sent forth). Barnabas is the one who seeks out Saul in Damascus and brings him to Antioch. Here both Saul and Barnabas have hands laid upon them and are sent by the Holy Spirit. In Acts chapter 14, they are now referred to as apostles, called and sent by the Holy Spirit, and bearing the new title and ministry of apostle. Whilst I

27

share a serious concern about some of those in the Church who call themselves apostles, their presence in no way negates the Word of God concerning apostles and apostleship today. Such men as C T Studd and Hudson Taylor, called and sent with a burning fire to deliver the Word of God and with an empowering of the Holy Spirit which fulfilled the Word of God in them, serve as examples. Such a call and gifting is still available in the Church.

Perfection in Jesus' Return?

There is also, of course, a group who believe that gifts continue. Generally, the belief held within this group is that the return of Jesus, being the culmination of all things, is the time of perfection spoken of by Paul in 1 Corinthians chapter 13, and is therefore the time when gifts, which are presumed to be imperfect, will no longer be needed.

Of course Paul, speaking to the believers in 1 Corinthians 1 verse 7, says, "You do not lack any spiritual gift as you eagerly wait for our Lord Jesus Christ to be revealed." Whilst agreeing about the continuation of gifts to present times and until Jesus returns, I can see no contextual evidence in 1 Corinthians which supports that particular view. I take the fact that the purpose of the gifts, of necessity remains as reason to believe that gifts also must remain to fulfil the enduring purposes of God in the lives of believers. In 1 Corinthians, Paul is not speaking about end times, but about order, growth, and in particular, maturity in the church. He speaks about gifts and their operation, their purpose and the context of their administration within and towards the love of God. When the Bible speaks of end times, the Greek word *telos* is used. It is normally part of a contextual phrase, such as "end times" or "end of the age", for example, Matthew chapter 24

If it is used alone – "the end" – then it is also held in a context. An example of this is Matthew 24 verse 14, where Jesus, speaking at length about the signs of the "end times", and of "His coming", concludes with the words, "then the end will come". If we return now to 1 Corinthians 13, we discover a very different context and, although the Greek word seems to be superficially similar to that used to when speaking of the end times, it is in fact a quite different word, *teleion* which is never used to describe "the end".

It seems difficult to prove from the scriptures then, that the work of the Holy Spirit came to an end either at the completion of the scriptures, or the end of what has become known as the Apostolic Era. Indeed many would argue that the era of the apostle is not over at all. The belief of many charismatics that the gifts will cease at the return of Jesus is , I believe true but if attempts are made to substantiate this on the basis of 1 Corinthians 13, this also fails to stand up to scrutiny. None of these theories, then, answer the question raised by 1 Corinthians 13: When does the perfect come? However, before I go on to consider the answer to that question, there is one more issue that must be addressed.

Chapter 3

Focus on Expression . . .

I began with a conversation between several venerable church leaders about the propriety of dancing in church. As happens so often, in this conversation the focus had shifted from the truth about the Holy Spirit to the appropriateness of apparent manifestations of the Spirit. It is too easy to become enmeshed in discussion about the sometimes rather strange, so-called manifestations or even genuine manifestations of the Holy Spirit, and to allow all too obvious errors and mistakes to distract us from the real issue of whether the Holy Spirit is still at work among God's people today.

Raising hands, dancing and clapping are all commonly found as expressions of worship in Charismatic congregations, so much so that one long-standing member of the church once confessed to me that she had thought that the expression 'charismatic' actually meant 'people who raise their hands when praising'! Even those who understand and exercise the gifts and ministries of the Holy Spirit can easily become misled by focus on external signs and expressions of worship. The truth is that expressions such as dancing or hand-raising, are not listed anywhere as gifts or ministries of the Holy Spirit. However, as much as our self-consciousness or our 'Britishness' might be uncomfortable with it, these expressions are completely Biblical, and could be described as natural outpourings of the joy of the Lord, which is a fruit of the Spirit and our strength.

Praying with raised hands is a practice found in both Old and New Testaments. For instance, in Psalm 63 verse 2, David has a glimpse of the power and glory of God and it has a profound effect as we see in verse 3:

> "Because your love is better than life, my lips will glorify you. I will praise you as long as I live, and in Your Name I will lift up my hands."

Whilst some might argue that David's expression of worship should hardly be regarded as the norm for Christians today, God didn't seem to mind as much as we do. As a matter of fact, David, even in the old covenant, walked very close to God, and I suspect knew more about true worship than most of his critics might admit.

In Psalm 134 we read:

> "Praise the Lord all you servants of the Lord, who minister by night in the house of the Lord. Lift up your hands within the sanctuary and praise the Lord."

Still there are cries that this is merely fanaticism; cries which hail, largely from a group of people who constantly claim to refer to the Bible as their guide. The Word of God strongly indicates that we should lift up our hands in praise to Him and that David, in moments of high praise to God, demonstrates his worship by lifting up his hands. Paul too, in 1 Timothy 2 verse 8, asks that, "All men everywhere, should pray, lifting up holy hands." Was David or Paul acting in a trite or unbiblical manner?

Another recent expression of worship is that people have been dancing in Church – a practice which has again caused eyebrows to be raised and comments to be made about such disgraceful behaviour in Church. You will remember the story I told about the group of church leaders discussing this very topic. I challenged them to respond to the Biblical command to "Praise the Lord with dancing." They had no response.

You can see the problem. Psalm 149 and 150 both say that we should "Praise the Lord with dancing." Lots of people try to duck the issue, some by saying that they are dancing in their hearts. Whilst I am aware that we don't take our lead from the world, it appears to me that other people dance with their legs.   If God says, "Preach the gospel," we would not argue that we should do it in our hearts but we would employ our mouths. Similarly, if the Word says, "Praise the Lord with dancing," is there an alternative understanding which we can bring to bear upon such a simple command of God? Is it right that some should raise such high criticism against those whose praise overflows in raising hands or dancing?

In Lamentations 5 verse 15, the writer equates the cessation of dancing with grief and slavery, creating the absence of joy:

> "Joy is gone from our hearts; our dancing has turned to mourning."

Now if joy is a fruit of the Holy Spirit, (Galatians 5 verse 22), is it unreasonable to expect that the expression of His presence with worshippers will include dancing? Is it such a disgrace, or is it the working of grace within us, which could free us sufficiently in Christ that we should praise Him with our whole being?

However, whilst hand raising and dancing are generally associated with forms of worship found in charismatic fellowships, as I said earlier, neither hand raising nor dancing are recorded as gifts of the Holy Spirit, but are just the smallest requirement of scripture concerning our praise. This then begs the question: if the Word asks such a simple thing, who then understands? Is it he who obeys the Word of God and finds joy in worship, or is it he who can come up with a clever theological argument which will support his position of intransigence?

Many maintain that the church should be a place of reverence and awe, silence and respect; a place of tradition and history. There is certainly some place for this in the church. We are not to take our relationship with God, or our worship of Him lightly. Our God is supremely mighty and powerful and a healthy reverence is necessary – as Proverbs chapter 1 verse 7 tells us, "The fear of the Lord is the beginning of wisdom." But in the Bible, God's people displayed their respectful response to God's awesome power in ways that were just as physical as the dancing and raised hands that they used to express their joyful response to his love and faithfulness.

Moses was a man who had powerful encounters with the Lord. In Exodus chapter 3, God appears to Moses from within a bush. Moses is told to take off his shoes because the place he is standing is Holy ground. I can't imagine an epidemic of shoe-removal breaking out in our congregations today, and yet when we seek to enter God's presence in worship, surely we are standing on Holy ground. Some response is required of us. Later, on Mount Sinai, Moses asked God to show him his glory, and in his graciousness, the Lord agreed to pass by Moses, as he hid in the cleft of a rock. What was Moses' response? "Moses bowed to the ground at once and worshipped." (Exodus 34 verse 8). This response of kneeling or bowing down in the presence of the majesty of God is found many times in the Bible. Some of the very churches which dismiss the idea of dancing or raising hands in worship will positively encourage kneeling during prayer or the eucharist. Can we have one part of God's word without the other?

In reality, all of these physical expressions of worship should be seen as manifestations of the response of our hearts towards the love, faithfulness, awesomeness and salvation power of the Lord. Many people who would not dream of raising their hands in worship will happily throw their hands in the air and even jump up and down when their favourite sports team wins an important match. Does God really deserve something less than the passion we would show for eleven men in matching shirts kicking a ball into a goal? If we can comfortably respond with stillness to the awe provoked by God's majesty, then it is only right that we can sometimes respond with movement to the joy provoked by God's great love. If that response is never in us, then perhaps we should question whether the joy is truly in us.

Perhaps, worthy of consideration too is the possibility that even some of those who through a Calvinistic conviction, predicate of a Sovereign God, may still be unable because of fear to submit to His ultimate authority and allow His continuing work upon the earth to move them.

Advocating more freedom in the way we worship is not, however, the same as saying that anything goes. Many who argue against the gifts of the Spirit in today's church cite examples of bizarre and ludicrous claims and practices amongst some charismatic Christians as evidence that all such manifestations are false, and perhaps even dangerous. I have of course witnessed several charismatic blunders, along with strange utterances, which I do not believe were conceived in the heart of the Lord, and I have witnessed some of the damage caused by words of counsel given in the Lord's name, but without wisdom or understanding. This however, in no way negates the Word of Truth, from which I have never discovered a single word of evidence to suggest that gifts have ceased. If charismatics do or say things which are wrong then, in love, their leaders should discipline them. False prophecies and exaggerated claims should be dealt with, but the Word of the Lord still stands. Cessationists caution against taking experience as our rule. In the same way, a wrong experience does not disprove the Word of God. If sick people are healed in the name of Jesus Christ and the Word of God does not say that this will happen, then we are untrue to the Gospel of Jesus Christ.

However, if the Word says that the sick are healed, then to deny it is to be untrue to the Word. Experience will constantly prove what is written but it should never amend it. The Word of God is not subject to men, nor to their interpretation. It is eternal, immutable and unswerving, being neither diminished by narrow mindedness, nor expanded by fantasy. It remains, of God, that which is written.

Chapter 4

Corinthians in Context . . .

In looking at the question of, "when the perfect comes", I want to examine the phrase in its context.   I will try to share some thoughts concerning, "the imperfect", and, "the perfect" and the purpose of gifts within this context.   We will ask the question of whether the Bible actually says that, "gifts will cease".

I do, of course, have a particular view, with which you may agree or disagree, but my prayer is that you might find something useful in discovering what the Word of God has to say on what is an important subject, and understand more of the Saviour, the Lord Jesus Christ and of His Holy Spirit, that we may become partakers by faith of every powerful act in love which the Holy Spirit might impart to us, that in the Church, the Lord Jesus might build and we might grow.

When Paul wrote his first letter to the Church at Corinth, it was to a Church which was struggling with the most horrific problems. Immorality, disorder, rebellion and misunderstandings were all part of the everyday life of the Church, and were problems which Paul sought to address. He refers to the church in Corinth as babies and implores them to grow up. He sees them as ignorant and disorderly and in addressing them, uses phrases such as, "Do you not know," and, "I would not have you ignorant." He seeks to establish orderly conduct in worship, and love and respect for one another.

In 1 Corinthians chapter 1 verse 7, Paul begins by acknowledging that the Corinthians have amongst them the working of every spiritual gift, but in verse 10, recognises that the problems in the Church are not being dealt with by gifts alone. Divisions and factions were then, as now, rife in the Church, with various apostles and leaders being followed, gifts and ministries being a contention, and unity having broken down. Paul makes his appeal in verse 10:

> "That you all agree with one another, so that there may be no divisions amongst you, and that you may be perfectly united in mind and thought."

This is Paul's first statement of his purpose in writing this letter. He wants to see unity and growth.

He continues from verse 17, with a discourse about wisdom and the power of the cross. The place of wisdom which is of God, not of men, is where we lay down our lives, fragmented as they are, in order to take up the life of Jesus Christ. It is to be joined by an abiding faith into that eternal hope, and we are to become partakers of His divine and loving nature, as we are baptised, not only with water by men, but also by the Holy Spirit, into the body of Jesus. Unity is not in being a Baptist or Anglican or Methodist, nor by following someone's particular religious regulation, but in belonging to the body of Christ by faith.

Recent developments have sought to bring together different denominations in order to promote unity. However, whilst some might feel that progress in unity is being made, Ecumenism will never be the instrument of baptism into the body of Jesus. This is still the work of the Holy Spirit, which happens where human precept cannot touch. Paul's first answer then to our question of unity is our relationship together in the body of Christ. In this body, Christ is both the wisdom and power (verse 24).

In chapter 2, Paul brings the wisdom and power of God to the Corinthians – firstly to the babies, with a demonstration of the power of God. In chapter 2 verses 4 and 5, he explains that this power comes from the Holy Spirit, and is demonstrated so that their faith might not rest in men, but in God. This, of course, contradicts the arguments of some who criticise gifts and would have us believe that gifts glorify men rather than God. Paul saw it the other way, that men might see the gift and believe God. He sees the gift, not purely as a means of scripture being written, but as a living dynamic towards people whose only hope was in the living God. Such a demonstration encouraged real faith as the Holy Spirit touched people's lives.

Obviously there was something different about the gifts which Paul displayed. The Corinthians' own gifts seemed to produce problems but Paul's produced faith and growth. He spoke and operated, not from a worldly understanding of power, but from the mature love of God which brought growth. He already knew the mystery that he reveals later in this letter: "If I have every gift and do not have love, then I have nothing and I gain nothing." (1 Corinthians 13 verses 1 to 3 abbreviated). Gain in Christ-likeness, for these immature Christians, was through the working of the gifts and powers of the Holy Spirit, but only in the context of the love of God. He had not chosen a superior or more excellent human wisdom, but rather a way which brought his own knowledge to nothing and brought him with fear and trembling to a total dependence on God – a more excellent way. He allowed his own knowledge and gifts to be brought to nothing, counting his richest gain as loss, for the sake of knowing Jesus and the power of his resurrection at work in him.

Next in chapter 2, Paul makes us aware that there are some who are more mature. To these, he does not offer a demonstration of power for the development of their faith but, withholding those gift ministries which he offers to the babies, he now comes up with something more appropriate for the mature. To these he brings a word of wisdom which overwhelms human wisdom. He describes this wisdom as a revelation by the Spirit of God of things which men have never seen. The power of the word which Paul now speaks is amazing. He speaks of things which the human eye has not seen, nor ear heard. He speaks of the deep things of God. To qualify this he says that we have received the Spirit of God who knows God's deepest thoughts, so that we might understand what God has freely given to us (chapter 2 verses 11 and 12). He culminates this remarkable chapter with this staggering and quite incredible statement: "You have the mind of Christ," knowing that which is beyond knowledge. Not just words of knowledge but the anointed mind and wisdom of Jesus, who is the Christ.

In Romans chapter 12, Paul again emphasises that power and wisdom are in the cross, available by the presentation of our bodies as living sacrifices, so that we might no longer be conformed to this world, but transformed. How? By the renewing of the mind, transforming it so that we have the mind of Christ. Then we will have knowledge of what God's will is; not just a word, but a mind revelation of the good and perfect, *teleion* will of God.

Look again at 1 Corinthians chapter 2. To whom is Paul addressing these staggering words of wisdom? He refers to them as, "the mature", or if we read the authorised version of the Bible, "them that are perfect". In the Greek we read, *"tois teleois"*, 'the perfect ones'. Paul actually describes these more mature Christians in Corinth as 'them that are perfect', but when he sees these men, he doesn't see them as being perfect as we would understand perfection. He sees for example, that they are not complete in their wisdom and therefore offers wisdom to them. But he does see them as mature, not because of their age, but because they have that close relationship with Jesus through his cross, even to the point of having the mind of Christ. Paul is setting the foundation for what is to follow. To the immature, the babies or children, who thought and spoke as he used to speak when he was a child, he brings a demonstration of power. To the mature, the adults, the perfect, he brings a message of wisdom concerning the mature, Holy Spirit relationship between God and man. I want to emphasise here that Paul uses this word, 'perfect', *teleion*, concerning those who are given to the will of God, united in the mature love of God, submitted to the wisdom of the cross and seeking not their own, but His kingdom.

In Ephesians chapter 4 and beginning at verse 12, Paul writes that gifted, mature, Holy Spirit officers in the Church are to:

> "Prepare God's people for works of service, so that the body of Christ may be built up until we all reach unity in the faith, and in the knowledge of the Son of God, and become mature, *(teleion),* attaining to the full measure of the fulness of Christ. Then we will no longer

be infants tossed back and forth by the waves, and blown here and there by every wind of teaching and by the cunning and craftiness of men in their deceitful scheming. Instead, speaking the truth in love we will in all things grow up into Him who is the Head, that is Christ. From Him the whole body, joined and held together by every supporting ligament, grows and builds itself up in love as each part, does its work."

Not only is this perfection of which Paul speaks attainable for men, but we are actually encouraged to aim for it, and be built up until we all attain to it. The theme which is beginning to develop in 1 Corinthians is that it is God's desire for us that through the work and power of the Holy Spirit, we are to be built up towards the aim of achieving the fullness of perfection and maturity in love, losing our childish infancy and becoming Christ-like. In fact there is another occasion in 1 Corinthians 14 verses 19 and 20, where Paul, after he has spoken about gifts in Chapters 12 and 13, says,

> "In the Church, I would rather speak five intelligible words to instruct others, than ten thousand words in a tongue. Brothers, stop thinking like children. In regard to evil be infants, but in your thinking be adults, *(teleioi)*."

The Authorised Version translates this word as "Perfect".

The mature apostle and teacher, not forbidding tongues, but encouraging their purpose and speaking of his own restraint from the gift, in deference to the need for love and maturity in the form of instructing the saints in their growth.

If we continue in 1 Corinthians we discover Paul again speaking to infants who need to grow, and again their divisions are a sign of their infanthood. Speaking of this growth, Paul reminds us that no man, no matter how gifted, can himself give growth to the church which is the body of Christ. True ministry of the Holy Spirit glorifies God, in that real growth and spiritual development come only from Him. 1 Corinthians 3 verse 7 says that "Only God gives growth".

Where then is man's involvement? Paul tells us in verse 5 that each is assigned a task. He describes his own part in the work as "nothing", saying: "I planted and Apollos watered"; "we have our purpose and will be rewarded"; "We are God's fellow workers." Men are involved in building the church but their involvement is rewarded by God, and so men have no claim over the church. The true building, being everything which will withstand the fire, and the field where growth takes place, belongs to God. "Do you not know that you are the temple of the Holy Spirit?" The man of God recognises who owns the property rights, and that the building is filled, not with worldly wisdom, irrespective of its spiritual disguise, but with the Holy Spirit. Paul's choice continues to be the cross which is the wisdom of God, not his own knowledge or his tongues or his superior revelation, so that the aim of achieving perfection might be fully met through his availability to the Lord in His work of building the church. This echoes the love of God in Christ who being by very nature God, did not count equality with God a thing to be grasped but became the humble obedient servant, even unto death on a cross.

Living to Grow . . .

Having spoken about the need to grow in the Spirit and to be built up in the Kingdom and having identified in chapter 3 the difference between what is precious in the building and what is worthless and only fit for burning, and who owns what, Paul now seeks to correct some potential misunderstandings about the Christian life. If we are to aim for perfection, finding maturity in love and having our minds renewed so that we have the mind of Christ, we must begin to apply Kingdom thinking in every area of our lives.

In chapter 5, Paul addresses the problem of immorality in the church, taking a strong disciplinary line. Many have sought to criticise those who seek to teach and operate in the love of God as being too soft where discipline is involved. According to chapter 5 verse 12, we are to judge the church but not the world. Later in chapter 11, when Paul speaks about the Lord's Supper, he expects that we will judge ourselves with the mind of Christ. Our failure to do so has caused some to become ill and some to die and because of this we profane the body of Christ and bring ourselves under the judgement of God. In our churches today, we debate at length whether or not the unbeliever or the unbaptised should even be present when we share the Lord's Supper, but in reality we ought to examine ourselves, who, by faith and the new birth profess to be partakers of the body and blood of Jesus and yet act in such a contrary manner.

"Are you ignorant?" Paul asks. "Do you not know?" This phrase appears six times in chapter 6. He expects that the mature ('perfect') Christian will have a knowledge of God which will be worked out in a changed lifestyle and especially with regard to the way we judge ourselves and the Church. He reminds us that one day we will be the ones who will judge angels. This understanding of judgement and discipline in the context of the cross and the forgiveness of Jesus is vital to our life, growth and ministry within the body of Christ.

Lifestyle continues to be Paul's theme in chapter 7, but now in the context of marriage. Marriage and divorce is a serious issue in the Church and improper conduct is a robber of spirituality. In verse 35, Paul shows that he wants nothing to come in the way of our devotion to God:

> "I am saying this for your own good, not to restrict you, but that you may live in a right way in undivided devotion to the Lord."

Paul does not give us harsh rules to bind us up, but rather instructions that, if followed, will release us into a place of freedom where we can devote ourselves to the Lord with undivided attention, not distracted by the consequences of our sinful actions.

However, as we move towards maturity, we are not to damage others with our freedom. In chapter 8, Paul speaks to the Corinthians about eating food sacrificed to idols, saying that he would rather never eat meat again if eating it would cause his brother to sin. Paul knows that idols are nothing in the world, and therefore eating food that has been sacrificed to them makes us no nearer or farther away from God. It is interesting that while this knowledge is not sin but rather a gift knowledge which frees us in Christ from the bondage of religion and of other people's weaknesses, Paul nevertheless in chapter 8 verses 9 and 10 tells us that by such knowledge it is possible to destroy a brother.

There is a need to move to the place where our knowledge is grounded in a love which is beyond knowledge, which Paul speaks about in Ephesians chapter 3 verses 18 and 19: "love that surpasses knowledge." Knowledge which is rooted and grounded in the love of Christ, has a fuller breadth and length and height and depth. It is better able to judge and discern in the Church. Knowledge alone can puff us up so it is better to love God and be known by God and then we can really know just as we are known. Those who are mature can hold back their counsel, their knowledge, their revelation and their tongue, so that someone may be helped and not destroyed.

Restraint in gift ministry is an important factor of our worship so that decency and order might prevail. In 1 Corinthians 14 verses 19 and 20, we have already seen that Paul says that he would rather speak five intelligible words than ten thousand in tongues, and that in our thinking we should be mature, perfect. Paul tells the Corinthians to exercise the mind of Christ in their thinking and speak in a way that builds the Church or be silent and hold their tongues. Although he has the rights of an apostle, Paul does not exercise his rights if they would do damage to others.

We partake together with one another of the same Jesus. We must be builders and not destroyers; this has always been God's purpose in the church. In chapter 10, Paul begins to look at the history of the Israelites. They all passed under the same cloud, ate the same spiritual food, and drank the same spiritual drink from the rock, which was Christ. Paul is also speaking of the body into which we are all baptised. Just as Israel sinned and God was not pleased, we too at one time were led astray by dumb idols, but now God, who reveals by his Spirit, speaks a different wisdom. In chapter 10 verse 17, we are now asked to be partakers with one another in the body and blood of Jesus.

At the end of chapter 10, Paul leads us to the point of what he has been saying. In verse 32 we read,

> "Do not cause anyone to stumble, even as I try to please everyone in every way. For I am trying to please everyone in every way so that many might be saved."

Paul's continuing theme is the building and growth of the Church in love. He is prepared to give up everything except the Lord's honour, but including his own honour, (chapter 4 verse 10), for the sake of seeing the Church grow in Christ. He is aware of the work of the Holy Spirit as being the only possible means of growth, but recognises man's involvement. Along the way, he points to the various landmarks of unity: revelation, kindness, patience, knowledge and wisdom. He saves the word "love" for a very special place in chapter 8 verse 1, where he says, "knowledge puffs up, but love builds up". Paul isn't speaking against knowledge, but pointing out how it is to be manifest in the Church. If we are aiming to grow towards maturity then our knowledge must be spoken in the love of God, constantly making that love our aim. Chapter 14 verse 1 says that we should make love our aim and objective, and that we should also desire spiritual gifts. At the end of chapter 12 we are told to eagerly desire the greater gifts, and there is a more excellent way. Literally, this is the way which cannot be measured, *uperbole*, the way of love. Love, which itself bears all the marks of patience and kindness, never fails. It is the bond of perfection, *teleiotetos*, which, in Colossians 3 verses 14 and 15, makes the body to be one. It is the answer to Jesus' final prayer where in John chapter 17 verses 20 to 26, Jesus, praying for the Church, asks His Father for their love and that they be "made perfect, *teleioo*, in unity".

Lord, teach us the way of love.

The Way of Love

Chapter 13 of 1 Corinthians is aptly placed between chapters 12 and 14. Often read at weddings or to speak about "What love is", the chapter is regularly read alone and therefore out of context. The theme of 1 Corinthians is consistent throughout the whole letter, but if we are going to try to divide it into paragraphs or chapters, then the immediate comment of chapter 13 begins, at the very least, at the beginning of chapter 12 and continues to the end of chapter 14. If we compare 1 Corinthians 12, 13 and 14 with Ephesians chapter 4, which we looked at earlier, there are remarkable similarities. It begins with the Church being brought together in unity through baptism in water and the Spirit into one Lord, one faith and one body. The building up by the manifestation of the Holy Spirit, towards the one goal, which is perfection and maturity in the love of God as portrayed in Jesus, becomes, in a more realistic way, loving and preferring one another.

As we look at 1 Corinthians chapter 13 in relationship with its adjoining chapters, what we are seeing is not a chapter about human love which is to be read at weddings, but a focus on the bond of perfection for every gift, ministry, service and servant in the Kingdom of our God. We see a dynamic of the Holy Spirit which, when we grasp it, focuses our hearts on the real purpose of gifts of the Holy Spirit. It reveals the platform for their operation, and becomes the unfailing, abiding, ceaseless embrace of their continuity and the sole and valid reason why they can be stopped or withheld. It tells of why we should have such gifts and yet speaks of something overwhelmingly better, towards which the church is moving: *agape*, the love of God which is in Christ Jesus – our aim, most excellent, all consuming, all embracing, the bond of our perfection and that which caused the only begotten Son of God to live and die and rise again for us.

A brief look at the three chapters will give us an indication of where the church begins and where it is expected to change. We see the direction marked out. In chapter 12, the church is a body with many different parts, but fragmented and disjointed. There are contentions concerning gifts and ministries, and disunity is rife. Paul exhorts people to be one, while acknowledging the differences of gifts and ministries as necessary if the people are to be different parts of a whole body.

In chapter 13, he looks at the way of love which will bind all of these gifts and people together to create that functioning body of which he speaks. Gifts are the manifestation of the Holy Spirit in a fragmented, dysfunctional, immature body for its growth; a gift to men from God who is from age to age, unchanging love. Gifts then, without this love, are nothing. Without love as their aim they are aimless and pointless, a noisy gong or a clanging symbol.

At the opening of chapter 14, Paul says we should follow the way of love and eagerly desire spiritual gifts. He gives the impression that the building which is being created is called love and that the bond which holds it all together is love, but the tools of our trade are gifts and ministries, services for the completion of the work. Ephesians 4 says that gifts are the equipment of the saints for their works of service. Continuing in 1 Corinthians chapter 14, Paul speaks about our conduct in worship in the congregation of the saints. He is, however, still speaking about the operation of gifts in love, the aim of which was stated at the beginning of this chapter. Chapter 14 then shows in a practical way how we can show off our genuine love, not our gift, thereby exalting the Lord who is greater than our gift. If we asked the question: "Which is the greater, the tools or the house? Which is the aim of our building?" we would probably conclude with Paul that the greatest is love.

Chapter 5

I am nothing ...

"If I speak in tongues or have a prophetic gift, can understand mysteries or have a gift of knowledge or have such faith that I can move mountains, if I am generous and give all my money to the poor and become a martyr for the faith, but have not love, **I AM NOTHING"**. Paul has shown us that gifts, without love as the aim and the bond, amount to nothing in the building process because they are the tools, not the material and not the end product. We desperately need the correct tools properly cleaned and honed in order that the job might be properly done, but the purpose, the gain, the aim, the whole point of what we are doing is the building and its completion.

As a young apprentice to my trade, I recall arriving on my first day with my new white overall and a small assortment of brand new tools. I hadn't much idea what I should do with the tools, but to me they looked good. I later discovered that none of the tools were much use, since tradesmen rarely use the tools which you buy for DIY work. I was encouraged to seek better tools. At the end of the first day, I packed my tools away – they hadn't stood up to the job very well – put on my coat, and was setting off to catch the bus home.

"Aren't you taking your overalls off?" asked Les. I was shy and didn't answer. I wanted to keep them on so that everyone could see that I was working. I felt that I was a man (aged 15!) of importance and I wanted to look the part. Cyril helped me out. "Let him keep them on.

It's his first day." The next day, they explained to me that wearing dirty overalls on the bus wasn't such a good idea.

Later I learned that whilst the tools and overalls were important in their own right, my employers were much more concerned that I learned my trade to their high standard. This meant training, college, mistakes, successes, having to do the jobs which no one else wanted, becoming part of the team, learning what needed to be done next and how far you could take something. I learned what materials were useful for what function and while learning everyone else's skills, I developed my own understandings. For six years as an apprentice it seemed that everything that happened was intended to make me a skilled tradesman and so it was, but the higher intention was the maintenance of the huge number of hospital facilities, for which the area hospital management committee had responsibility.

Of course there were different tools for different jobs, and learning which tools were appropriate for which job was important. Now, as a Christian minister, I sometimes get involved with church maintenance work. I find that the grace needed to allow the young men in the church to help with the maintenance work is not easily found. I would rather do it myself – it's quicker and simpler and I know that it would be done properly. The difficulty I have is that tradesmen taught me. But, if I can allow those young men to make their mistakes and train myself to look at the bigger picture, not only will the maintenance continue, but they will learn skills which they can use in their own homes, where they have wives and families. It's a more difficult but more excellent way. Besides, if I stay behind to clear up, I can also just tweak the mistakes so that it looks a bit better.

In the Church we need the tools and the skills, but much more we need the bigger purpose of the love of God. We may have all the gifts – the equipment – but we need the mortar – the love – and the picture of the finished product. Without these we cannot begin to build. Gifted people in the Church often appear powerless. Even though they manifest gifts of the Spirit, there doesn't seem to be much real growth around them. A skilled man using the best tools and having mortar and a purpose, will build the best building. If you took his tools off him he would probably make a better job than most using just his skilled hands. Without a purpose or plan, and without mortar, he would never get started. He would finish up in the unenviable position of guarding a pile of stones, the plight of some disillusioned church leaders or evangelists, who Jesus called to be fishers of men and now have a job keeping an aquarium.

I once heard someone describe a man's ministry as "like a mighty oak". The one who was speaking paused, then added, "very impressive to look at, but nothing grows under it." Selfish ambition is a killer in the church, resulting in leaders and others who are constantly looking for a platform on which they can shine. The promotion of a man's ministry has a place in the church only in order that he be built up and built in. I am not speaking of those who labour tirelessly in the Lord and receive their proper wages, but I was appalled a short while ago to see a well-known teacher in a big auditorium appealing for money, loading false guilt on people that they might support his ministry. A thuggish armed guard carried the huge trunks of money. Would they shoot someone who tried to steal from them? Some leaders seem to believe that they are obviously the most anointed and seek every opportunity to take the biggest and best place on every occasion. Often there is a tight control over all the genuine ministry opportunities, because the leader believes he can do it better.

In Joshua chapter 6, Israel conquered Jericho when God told them to act all together as one band walking around the city, and then together blowing all their trumpets. No one was to blow his own trumpet! But more seriously, the Lord had told them not to touch the devoted things, the gold and precious things which were used in service in the temple at Jericho. Achan, son of Carmi, took some of those things for himself and hid them in his tent and because of this the Lord withdrew His favour from the Israelites. They made their own plan to conquer Ai, knowing that they were strong and believing that God was in their plan. Of course the Israelites lost at Ai. They came before the Lord, and God told Joshua that Israel had sinned. Everyone was held to account. Eventually, Achan was found and put to death. It may seem unfair that God stopped the whole of Israel in their tracks over one man's sin, but he expects us to discern and safeguard and oversee one another, encouraging each other to good works. "Do you not know that you are the temple of the Holy Spirit?" Paul asks. In our midst are the precious, devoted things. They belong to the Lord. The gift ministries given into the hands of ordinary men and women are for each one severally to serve the Lord. They are not to be buried in the tent of the Pastor, or to be the property of the most vocal leader or charismatic member.

In John's gospel, chapter 4, Jesus encounters the woman from Samaria at the well at Sychar. The disciples had gone to get some food and when they returned, they offered Jesus something to eat, but He said to them in verse 32, "I have food to eat, which you know nothing about." Jesus continues at verse 34, "My food is to do the will of him who sent me and to finish the task." Food, in the kingdom of God, is not listening to a good sermon as we have long believed, but to do the will of Him who sends us and to finish the task. In 1 Corinthians 11, Paul speaks to the Corinthian Church about the Lord's Supper where he says that their meetings do more harm than good and they selfishly reject one another and eat without consideration for others. Ananias and Sapphira died because of this in Acts chapter 5. Here in 1 Corinthians 11, Paul is speaking of physical food, but he is also speaking of profaning the body of Christ. "We all partake of the one loaf," he said in chapter 10 verse 17. He is speaking of the food which is Jesus; food which Jesus says is to do the will, in love, of Him who sends us, and to finish the task. If I hold a monopoly on gifts of the Spirit, if I seek to build "My ministry" instead of the body of Christ, then I withhold from the people their share of the loaf, their food, the devoted things. Paul says, "Some people have become sick and some have fallen asleep" – they died.

In our fellowship was a man who is now retired, but continuing to serve the Lord in his retirement; a man of Holy Ghost faith, who served as a deacon. I had had a sore wrist for some time and so I asked if someone might come and pray for me. After some time, this man and his wife came forward and as he took hold of my hand, he said quietly, "I don't think I should be doing this." I understood his love and concern for me but I was a bit perplexed about that comment. After he had prayed, he returned to his seat and my wrist was no better. We arrived at the time for the breaking of bread, which would normally be towards the end of the meeting, but on this occasion we had it earlier in the meeting. Two giggling girls about thirteen or fourteen years old came to the front and stood in front of me. I looked at them, wondering if they wanted prayer for something.

They nudged each other, saying, "You tell him," "No you tell him." One did speak eventually in a very shy and broken manner: "We think God has said that we should pray for your wrist." They then stood for a moment, looking as if they were about to be struck by lightning. I did not know whether to laugh or weep, but I invited them to pray. Upon their simple prayer, the pain went immediately and has never since returned. Praise the Lord for His healing and His word of truth. He gives gifts, severally as He wills, and not to the best and oldest minister. When I spoke later to the faithful deacon, he was beside himself with joy for those young people. He continues to be a skilled builder, laying foundations, planting seeds and encouraging others to come into the field and take up the work. I have noticed that for such a skilled man of faith, he sometimes seems apparently unable to do anything right by himself, and always needs someone with no skill to do it better. Yet as he teaches and preaches the Truth about Jesus, many people around him seem to be being saved and growing in grace. Remarkable, isn't it?

Selfish ambition fails to reveal effective power in church building, but also endangers the whole Church and can halt the movement of a fellowship, a town or even a nation, and it has been the cause of death. A bricklayer with a trowel uses it to apply the mortar or to cut bricks. Without love, cutting the bricks is the only alternative.

If there is a gift of healing then that manifestation is for the common good, (1 Corinthians 12 verse 7). That doesn't just mean that everyone benefits from healing, but from the entire manifestation of the Holy Spirit. We are all partakers. This is because the building work of the Holy Spirit is changing our character to make us more like Jesus, to attain to the perfection found in Him. Therefore, if I am younger, or less honourable in the body, I need more Holy Spirit work within me. I need more of His unchanging Love changing me, and more opportunity for this grace to work in my life towards others. Who ought first to partake of the loaf? The strong? The greedy? The loud? Paul says that we should not eat before those who have had nothing at home. Who should be more honoured? The faithful deacon, who I mentioned earlier, is secure in his relationship with the Lord, sufficient to be able to release to others the encouragement of being the one who lays hands on the sick, and allow the Lord to do the healing. In Exodus chapter 15 verse 26, we learn that God has said, "I am the Lord, who heals you." The gift of the Son of God, the living Word, is ministered to us from a Father's heart which burns with passion for the Church to be formed. This is the very basis of the Father's giving, eternal love, outside of which there is no real gift, only stolen devoted things, the fading and sullied glory of a man.

Chapter 6

In Part . . .

"For we know in part and we prophesy in part."
It sounds as though there is only part of a gift
available. Many people have sought to argue
that prophecy was never like that in the Old
Testament. The prophet said, "Thus says the
Lord," and it was thus. The false prophet was
put to death. Well, it may sound remarkably
naïve to make the comment, but we are no
longer in the Old Testament. We are in the New
Covenant of the slain Lamb of God and people
of the resurrection life, into which rebel sinners,
unchurched, unskilled, and even uncouth are
born again as "new born babes," a phrase which
Paul chooses to use in 1 Corinthians 3
concerning the Christian church who were

undeniably gifted and yet getting it wrong. He says in 1 Corinthians 14 verse 31, "You can all prophesy, in turn, so that everyone might be instructed." No stoning, just correction in the way in which prophesy should be administered.

Of course Saul of Tarsus, the Pharisee and scholar, would know better than any of us today that this could never have happened under the oversight of the Sanhedrin. Obviously Paul, the Christian apostle to the gentiles who were once far off but were, in the New Covenant, brought near by the blood of the cross, was expecting something different. Jesus had already pioneered this with uneducated fishermen, a thief for a treasurer and a whole strange bunch of people who, quite frankly, might be politely asked to leave most of our Sunday services. On one occasion in Matthew's gospel, chapter 7 verse 36, Jesus attended the house of Simon the Pharisee and was reclined, eating his meal when a sinful woman burst in. She didn't seek permission, was obviously a known hooker, and wailed and wept so much that her tears fell down onto Jesus feet. There she washed his feet, drying them with her hair. How embarrassing! Then she broke open a bottle of perfume – maybe not the expensive nard which the sister of Martha used, but perhaps the cheap scent she used to freshen up after work. Simon was incensed. Jesus, however, loved her. We don't know who this woman was, but I think it may have been Mary Magdalene, who when she went to the empty tomb, realised that the one stood before her was Jesus as he spoke her name. In Revelation chapter 1 verse 5, John speaks of the one who has loved us and washed us from our sins in His own blood and made us to be kings and priests to serve His God and Father. To Him be glory and power forever and ever, amen.

God has obviously put extraordinary things into the grasp of ordinary people. With the new birth, comes entry into the kingdom of the Son of God, but we arrive as babies not adults. Every good and perfect gift comes from the Father of lights, in whom there is no shadow of turning, according to James chapter 1 verse 17. The gift is not in part, but is perfect (*teleios*), for the recipient who is not, in order that the Father of light, (*phos*), *illumination or manifestation*, might manifest himself amongst His people and bring them in love from their imperfection to His perfection, although there are different manifestations from the Father in every believer.

Paul, knowing how we are joined in Jesus to become the body of which Jesus spoke and for whom He prayed, continues to use the metaphorical body to illustrate what he is saying. 1 Corinthians 12 verse 12 and following, describes how the body, though one, is made of several parts. Each part is given equality in importance, because, whatever its function, it is equally a part of the same body.

> "The body is a unit and though it is
> made up of many parts, they form
> one body. So it is with Christ."

One body, many parts, baptised by one Spirit into membership of His body, whether Jews or Greeks, slaves or free, all given of the one Spirit to drink. To make a body you need different parts. We may consider some parts more vital to us than another. God begins with equal importance and Paul expounds this. In order that the body is seen to be equal he begins to say that less honourable parts should be given more honour so that there is no recognisable difference in importance in the different parts of the body. Of course there are different personalities and ministries but none is more important than another. Because God has no favourites, he will treat with favour those who lack it, in order that no one is favoured overall. He wants us to be one in Christ.

In 1 Corinthians 12 verse 25, Paul says that there should be no division, but that each part should have equal concern for each other. Some have said that gifts are divisive. It seems that Paul is saying that gifts don't divide, but that division is in the heart of man, and this is the very thing which God needs to deal with if the church is going to grow, so he asks that we love and regard every one as equal, bound together by love. The difficulty which we have in achieving unity and growth within the body of believers doesn't arise from the manifestation of different gifts but from our lack of love towards one another.

God gives gifts which are good and perfect to be operated in the powerful, brooding love of the Holy Spirit, who, at the beginning of creation, hovered above the chaos of the unformed earth until the Word, who was in the beginning, spoke light (manifestation) into being and by His Word formed all things. In the Word all things are made, and in that revelation of the Holy Spirit, (the good and perfect gifts, from the Father of lights), chaos is brought to nought and the order of God's new creation is brought about. We need this love work of the Holy Spirit to bring order into the chaos of our churches and relationships so that we can operate effectively in God's gifts, not allowing division to limit our growth and destroy the effectiveness of our witness to the unbeliever.

In 1 Corinthians 12 verse 27, Paul tells us that, "We are the body of Christ and members of it in part." This could seem to imply that our membership of the body is partial or incomplete, but the literal translation says "members in particular", which gives a different accent to what he is saying. In the Greek we read two phrases, (*en melos*), and (*ek merous*). These phrases are both on occasions translated "in part", but they have different meanings. Imagine a fruit cake. If someone gives you a slice, you have a part of it that is a representation of the whole thing, containing a portion of all the ingredients that make up the complete cake. By the same token, each separate ingredient is also a part of the cake, even though each one is completely different from the other. With one ingredient missing, the whole cake would not be complete. Now, when Paul speaks about the body, he is saying that we are each a portion of the whole body, representative of everything which God has recreated us to be in Christ like a slice of the cake. He is also saying that we are a limb or an organ – a particular part of the body, like an ingredient in the cake. It is too easy to apply only the second interpretation here (that of being a limb or an organ with only one purpose), and miss the other implication that we are also a representative section, or slice of the body.

Paul goes on to speak of the parts in this way: "God has appointed some to be apostles, some prophets, some teachers, some workers of miracles and those having gifts of ...." etc. The parts are people, not gifts. They are gifted people, but the 'in part' refers to the people who operate in the gift, not the gift itself, because in God and in his gift there is no division, and no variation or shadow of turning, and as we have seen, the phrase 'in part' when applied to the people, need not necessarily mean division or separation or a partial membership of the body. So, in fact, neither the people nor the gift is divided or incomplete.

It is slightly strange that both Greek phrases are translated "in part" since in Greek the word "*ek*" (of "*ek merous*") is much more reasonably translated alone as "from", or "out of" rather than "in". So that *from* one part we have prophecy, *from* another part we have tongues. If there is no division of the gift, then it is perfectly reasonable to say that "from parts", not "in part", we have a manifestation of a gift, so that our current experiences of the gifts are not actually partial, but instead, coming *from* part of the whole gift. In Ephesians chapter 4 verse 16, we discover that,

> "From the Head, the whole body joined and held together, by every supporting ligament, grows and builds itself up in love as each part, (*merous*), does its work."

Towards what? "Until we have unity of faith and of the knowledge of the Son of God, becoming the mature, full stature of perfection in Jesus."

In 1 Corinthians 13 verse 9, it says that, "We know in part and we prophesy in part," (*ek merous* – from part). Of course we prophesy from the place of our imperfection, but we also prophesy from that part of the body which is gifted. Later Paul deals with this, in chapter 14 verse 29, where it appears that the totality of the gift is distributed, (in chapter 12, "severally as He wills"). He clearly expected that there would be a number of prophets. After all, he started in Antioch where there were several prophets – this is new covenant life, not the fading glory of the old. He exhorts that, "Two or three prophets should speak." Where do you find two or three prophets in a Jewish congregation before the time of Jesus? He then says, "The others should weigh carefully what is said." The others? How many prophets might there be in one fellowship? Back at the time of Pentecost, in Acts chapter 2 verse 17, Peter said, "This was prophesied by the prophet Joel." We can uphold the Old Testament as our test for the New, knowing that one of those testable Old Testament prophets has spoken this:

> "In the last days I will pour out my Spirit on all flesh. Your sons and daughters will prophesy, your young men will see visions and your old men dream dreams. Even upon my servants will I pour out my Spirit and they will prophesy."

Does he really mean all his servants? That's what the tested Old Testament prophet says.

Does he intend that in the Church all can prophesy, bringing their part to the congregation of the reborn ones so that they might all grow and be built towards that perfection which is in Christ Jesus? That's what he says.

Paul also says that "We know in part." It's true that if we could somehow network our minds, we would probably know more together than we do apart. The Lord though, does not want a better sum of our human understanding, but the transformed, renewed, submitted mind of Christ. Remember Ephesians 3 – we can, in the love of God, have a knowledge which is beyond knowledge (*epignosis*). We can see that we are, "of part" – we clearly have not yet achieved the mind of Christ – but there seems to be a solution here in the love-bound ministry of the gifts of the Holy Spirit. Maybe this is the more excellent way of which Paul speaks, not limited or partial, but beyond measure, beyond limit.

Jesus said, in John chapter 14 verse 12. "I tell you the truth." When Jesus says that, Christians need not debate what he says.

> "Anyone who has faith in me will
> do what I have been doing. He
> will do even greater things because
> I go to my Father."

Yes, that's what he said. Some Christians, mostly those who do not believe that gifts are for today, but also some who perhaps seek to apologise for the weakness of the Churches' representation, have said that this refers to "more things" (as in a greater number), because there are more Christians. Jesus actually said "any**one**", and "**he** will do . . . **greater** things." Jesus was expecting a Church of power because He was going to the Father. He speaks of pouring out the Holy Spirit and prays that we will become one, but is He only speaking of this?

Again Paul's letter to the Ephesians, in chapter one, speaks the incredible. Yet if we can grasp it by faith it is amazing. I paraphrase so that you can see what I believe Paul is saying. Verse 17 – *I keep asking the Father of lights, of all Spiritual revelation, to give you the wisdom which sees the purpose of God from its beginning to its end so that your knowledge of Him may not be limited but expanded in the mind of Christ. I pray that the Father of lights, of revelation, of manifestation, might Illuminate your Spiritual sight, opening your eyes to see with all of that wisdom and knowledge, the eternal abiding hope which I have invested in your life and how rich and glorious an investment that is becoming in you and all those who believe. There has never previously been anything like this in the whole history of mankind, because previously, the Father had never exerted such power, such love, such compassion, as that which He exerted when He raised His beloved Son, slain for the wickedness of men, from the deepest depth of hell to the highest height and Glory of heaven. There he now reigns eternally over every power, still working in you that same power, and He has become head of the fragmented disjointed body, that in Him we might become the bride, the glory of the Almighty God. Therefore, since He is appointed Head over everything concerning the Church, His body will be filled with everything of Him in every way possible.*

"Greater things" means more things, yes, but something new is at work, never available whilst Jesus walked the earth because it had not been seen. We can call it "Resurrection Power".

In James chapter 3 verse 13, the wisdom for which Paul earnestly prays on behalf of the Corinthians, comes with humility, in doing good deeds. This spiritual quality is active not passive. Wisdom produces practical humility. Paul then goes on to say that,

"selfish ambition, envy, disorderly conduct is of the devil, but" (verse 17) "the wisdom that comes from heaven is first of all pure then peace loving, considerate, submissive, full of mercy and good fruit, impartial and sincere. Peace makers who sow in peace will raise

a harvest of righteousness."

This is the growth that God wants: a mature, righteous harvest; a bride without the spot of youth or the wrinkle of old age, but mature, vibrant and radiant in His love. James says that this wisdom is impartial, without partiality or uncertainty or ambiguity. This was the very gift which Paul knew the Corinthians needed to be manifest in their partial, (*ek merous*), body, in order for the love of God to be released – a gift which would not be self seeking, which would take down the walls of division by its pure, gentle, humble impartiality, and which would not be self seeking or rude. This was the dynamic which was needed by those whom God was maturing in love. Walls could go. Two could become one in love. That which was "in part", could become whole. The most excellent way.

Chapter 7

Will cease . . .

So when will gifts cease?

This is the question to which everyone is seeking an answer, but I would like to ask something else first. Does the Bible actually say that gifts will cease? If we look at the variations of translation of 1 Corinthians 13 verse 8, then we begin to see a certain amount of disagreement concerning exactly what is being said. For example the AV says, "Prophesies will fail"; the RSV says, "Prophesies shall pass away "; the NEB says, "Their work will be over"; and the NIV says, "They will cease". Are they worn out, worked out, retired or dead?

If we look at the next phrase, it concerns the gift of tongues. The AV, RSV and NEV say that they will cease, but the NIV says they will be stilled. This is because the Greek word concerning the stilling of tongues is different than the one used for the stilling of prophecy or knowledge.

Perhaps a more detailed look at these words would be helpful. First of all concerning tongues, the Greek word is *pausontai*, which translates almost as it sounds: "Will be paused". In fact, according to the lexicologists, there is also embodied within this word the idea of an outside involvement in the pause. Perhaps if we said "Tongues will be restrained", it might be easier to understand.

Another possible interpretation might be, "You will be able to hold or control your tongue."

One reason for saying this is that the Greek word, *pauo,* which is the root from which our word is derived, when used on other occasions, does not normally denote a permanent enforced cessation. For example in Luke 11 verse 1, Jesus was praying. When He ceased, *epausato,* one of His disciples said, "Lord teach us to pray." If what the translators say is right (and there appears to be differences amongst them) then this would not have been the beginning of prayer in the Lord's Prayer, but the end. In fact Jesus, far from ceasing to pray, then taught His disciples the most powerful prayer lesson ever taught.

So does Paul say that tongues would be stopped, or rather that we should control our tongues? In 1 Peter we get a different feel for the meaning of the word. Peter writes that whoever loves life and would see long days must restrain, (*pauosato*) his tongue from evil speech. This is not an enforced cessation of evil speech; rather it is the restraint of that which James says is the hardest member of our body to bridle. James chapter 3 verse 2 tells us that, "Whilst we all stumble in many ways. If anyone is never at fault in what he says, he is a perfect, (*teleios*), man." James continues with that famous passage about the tongue and that which we looked at earlier about wisdom. There are many other similar references, none of which refer to an enforced cessation but all of which imply stopping voluntarily. If this is the normal use of the word, why on this occasion in 1 Corinthians would it be interpreted differently from every other occasion?

If we look at this in its context of 1 Corinthians 12, 13 and 14, we can see where it fits and what is actually being said. In chapter 12, Paul speaks of the fragmented but multi-gifted body, where gifts without love are not doing the work of building which they ought. Chapter 13 speaks of the most excellent way, the way of love, the way of maturity, the way of perfection. In Chapter 14, Paul begins with a lengthy request that for the sake of the Church and more especially the unbeliever, we ought to restrain our speaking in tongues. He does not indicate that there will be an absolute cessation. What he does ask is that we behave maturely, for the sake of others, for the sake of love and for the sake of order in the Church. In chapter 14 verse 5, he says that he wants everyone to speak in tongues. He then clarifies his own point about withholding, saying that he would rather that people bring a prophetic revelation, either as a tongue with an interpretation, or as a prophecy.

Without revelation, there is no "common good", which in chapter 12 Paul stated as the purpose of the gifts and the reason why the Holy Spirit was manifest. In 1 Corinthians 14 verse 6, Paul asks, "If I come to you, speaking in tongues, what good would I be to you?" He wants to bring to them the "good", the purpose of the gifts. In verse 13 he says, "If I pray in tongues, I pray with my Spirit but my mind is unfruitful." But the Spirit is reborn anew in Christ Jesus. The gift also is perfect from the Father of lights. What the Lord wants of us is fruitful, renewed transformed minds – this is where the work of grace is needed. Therefore, if I speak in tongues, I may edify my own mind with an understanding or a revelation to the inner man, but in the congregation, I need to be intelligible. Paul says that although he speaks in tongues more than anyone, in the meeting he would rather speak five intelligible words than ten thousand in tongues. The fact that he says, "I would rather" is significant. He obviously has a choice to make about where and when he administers the gift. For the sake of the unbelievers, tongues in the mature Christian should cease, or be stilled (*pausontai*) when appropriate.

At verse 22, Paul says that "tongues are a sign." I have seen this verse debated on many occasions. The question which best describes the crux of the debate is, "What on earth is he talking about?" If tongues are of no value to the unbeliever without interpretation, is Paul confused, as was once suggested by a friend of mine?

To begin with, signs are for unbelievers. Jesus spoke about this perverse generation requiring a sign, but they would only be given the sign of Jonah. Amazingly, even after Lazarus was raised from the dead, some did not believe. In fact, in keeping with the prophecy given to Isaiah, their eyes were blinded. Paul's prayer for the eye-opening wisdom of God in Ephesians chapter 1 gives us some insight into how the mystery of Christ was kept hidden until a time of revelation. We live in such a time. Jesus preached the opening of blind eyes. At his conversion, Paul was blinded and then his eyes opened only by a work of the Holy Spirit – a sign and a revelation as Jesus spoke into his life. When the disciples were commissioned by Jesus in Mark 16, they were told that signs would accompany them. In Joel's prophesy as referenced in Acts chapter 2, we are told that there would be signs and wonders in the heavens. The sign does not in itself accomplish a journey but points to the fact that the place to which we might travel actually exists, and if it is a road sign, for example, gives some indication of direction and distance. Signs are not for believers – we have our sign. Isaiah tells us that our sign is the sign of Immanuel, our God with us.

So then, tongues may get an unbeliever's attention in the sense that something unexpected is going on, but without prophetic revelation, the Holy Spirit explanation of the Word of God, the unbeliever might think that the speaker is out of his or her mind. In fact, if the dead are raised without the Word of God explained, people are probably as likely to be scared witless as they are to be saved. Therefore, ministry of the gifts in love is what is required, that we might grow and mature together in the grace and love of God.

With regards to what will happen to prophecy and knowledge, I said earlier that there were two words used in the Greek which are translated as "will cease". There have been differences in translation, reflecting differences of thought, which seems to be an indicator again that there is some division about exactly what the word means in that particular context. The Greek word used to describe what happens to both prophecy and knowledge is (in the singular concerning knowledge), *katargethesetai,* and (in the plural concerning prophesies), *katargetheontai*.   These are usually translated as "it will cease" (knowledge) and "they will cease" (prophecies).   This again translates with finality, but a look at the root of the word gives us further information.   The root is, *katargeo.* The major lexicologists translate this word as "render inactive".   A car can be rendered inactive by switching off the ignition, but it does not cause the car to cease to exist.   To render inactive does not presuppose that destruction is involved.

Paul uses this word twenty five times in the New Testament and so its use in different contexts by the same author is well documented. First of all, however we will look at what Jesus said in Luke chapter 13 verse 7.   Here, Jesus is speaking about a man who planted a fig tree which bore no fruit.   The complaint was that it was rendering the ground useless. The ground is still there giving up its goodness to the tree but no fruit is forthcoming. The ground is rendered inactive. It is encumbered, **katargeo,** because the tree is having an effect, taking up space and using up nutrients so that nothing else can be grown, but the gardener suggests that it can be made productive again.

Concerning prophesies, Paul says, in 1 Corinthians 14 verse 32, that the spirits of the prophets are subject to the control of the prophets. We may speak a prophecy, but if two or three have spoken then we may offer a ministry of a higher order which will render our gift inactive. This higher order ministry is the ministry of love, which comes with self control. The highest control is love and the aim is for the whole church to be built up in love. But, I hear you cry, what if God wants to say something prophetically important through me? I sincerely ask, has God never thought of that? Is not the Word and the revelation His that He might speak through the voice of less experience? In love, we can wait and weigh, holding our tongue or our prophecies for the sake of the love of God.

Paul also says in verse 31 that we can all prophesy in turn. That doesn't mean that my turn always has to be now. I know that there is sometimes an urgency of the prophetic which needs to be spoken now. Usually those revelations have an immediate necessity which is plain. If my revelation is an unnecessary intrusion then it is more likely to discourage than build. Have you ever come across the brother or sister who at every meeting has a 'word from the Lord', who after several hearings, sets people on edge as they hope that he will not interrupt the meeting again today, and then everybody cringes when it happens. Don't be the person who does that. We can, and sometimes should, render our gift inactive for the sake of love. It is a higher power and our gift must be brought under the control of it.

In 1 Corinthians chapter 1 verse 28, Paul said that God has chosen lowly and despised things to bring to nullify (*katargese*) the things that are. Again, this does not have the sense of things disappearing, but in the light of Jesus, worldliness is overwhelmed by a greater power and rendered inactive. You might think that the lowly and despised things cannot be greater than the wise, but the world's greatest wisdom does not come near to the wisdom of God. The lowly and despised things are God's choice – God's wisdom. If this is the wisdom which Paul offered to "the perfect", in 1 Corinthians in chapters 1 verse 6, then it must be a part of "the perfect" and not "the imperfect", which will be rendered powerless. If, then, someone has a revelation and someone else stands up who may not be as mature as we are, then a sign of our maturity and faith must be God's choice, God's wisdom, that those who by the world's standards may not be so honoured, might still have the prophetic revelation. We may be those who say that we believe the prophet Joel in Acts chapter 2, when he says that the Holy Spirit is poured out on all flesh. The real test of our belief will come when we can sit down and allow the younger, less mature men and women to prophesy. Do we really believe God?

Similarly with knowledge: does it cease? Or is it, like prophecy, designed to build up the body of Christ, until we reach a unity of faith and love, the full stature of perfection in the man, Jesus. If this is so, then there must come a point, where we as individuals are already built up, and where the equipment for building us is not so necessary, to the point where Paul says at the beginning of Ephesians chapter 4, that we should be taking up the maintenance program, maintaining the unity of the Spirit which has been built, in the one body – moving from the dependents to the dependable. Then we will not be the ones who, like children, are wanting all of the attention, but the wise, humble ministers of the ministry offices of Ephesians 4, overseeing and helping younger ones in their gift, and allowing our own ministries when necessary, to be rendered inactive by the more excellent power of love, the more excellent way.

It seems then, that the word 'cease' should not be interpreted as meaning that the gifts will disappear altogether, but rather that they will be stilled, according to the mature choice of the believer, so that we might prefer one another in love, allowing younger, less mature members of the body to be built up in the operation of their own gifts. This maturity in love is the perfection we aim for, and according to 1 Corinthians 13 verse 10, "when the perfect comes", it will render powerless, by subjection to itself, that which is imperfect.

Chapter 8

When I was a child . . .

In 1 Corinthians 11, Paul's appeal is still the same: grow up into the love of God. He uses this illustration of ordinary growing up. When I was a child, I talked, thought and reasoned like a child. My tongue, my soulish awareness and my logical understanding, were childish. Therefore, I uttered the words of a child. This of course is absolutely necessary for babies, but we don't continue our baby speech as we grow up, unless of course we are saying 'coochy coo' to a tiny baby. We shouldn't exercise the same sentiments when we are mature Christians as we do when we are childish and worldly. There are of course times when we need to see from a younger or even childish perspective, so that we can uplift and encourage, but they should not be the place of our dwelling. Sometimes we hold on to things and cannot let go in order to move on, but this is not the way of the mature. The writer of Hebrews points out in chapter 5 that those who are mature should not be learning, (recipients only of the benefit of the gift), but should become teachers. Anyone who lives on milk is not acquainted with the teaching about righteousness. But solid food is for the mature, who by constant use have trained themselves to discern good from evil.

Earlier, in 1 Corinthians 3 verse 1, Paul has already spoken of these things.

> "Brothers, I could not address you as Spiritual, but as worldly, as mere infants in Christ. I gave you

milk, not solid food, for you were not ready for it. Indeed, you are still not ready, you are still worldly. For since there is jealousy and quarrelling amongst you, are you not worldly? Are you not acting like mere men?"

Childishness and worldliness is demonstrated by their jealousy and quarrelling and lack of love towards one another. Obviously from the text, the subject of the quarrel was who ought to speak. I have seen the "whose turn is it to preach?" argument amongst leaders. It can be very destructive.

In 1 Corinthians 3 verse 16, Paul questions their ignorance about the fact that the body is the temple of the Holy Spirit. Here he issues a challenge to believers. He says that anyone who destroys this temple will be destroyed by God. Here Paul is not speaking of an individual being the temple, but rather the body of believers, those drawn together, baptised by the one Spirit and unified in the love of God. The destruction which Paul speaks of is the destruction of the unity of the Spirit, which has already been given to those who are in Christ. This is our unity, where we worship together as partakers of the one loaf, eating of the flesh of Jesus and drinking of His blood, where we worship in Spirit and in truth, not with arguments about whether we should sing hymns or choruses, but sharing in the genuine love of God. This is the temple, the household of faith, the living stones which are built together in love. It is that for which Jesus prayed in John chapter 17 verses 20 to 25:

"My prayer is not for them alone. I pray also for those who will believe in me through their message, that they may be one, Father, just as you are in me and I am in you. May they also be in us that the world might believe that you have sent me. I have given them the glory that you gave me, that they may be one as we are one. I in them, and you in me. May they be brought to complete unity to let the world know that you sent me and have loved them, even as you have loved me. Father, I want those you have given me to be where I am and to see my glory, the glory you have given me because you loved me, before the creation of the world.   Righteous Father, the world does not know you, I know you and they know that you have sent me.   I have revealed you to them, and will continue to make you known in order that the love you have for me may be theirs and that I myself may be in them."

Those who seek by their quarrelling to destroy this temple are in danger of being destroyed themselves. You may well say that you don't seek to destroy the temple of God, but if we remain in our infancy of thinking, our childish reason, which is based on the wisdom of men, holding onto logical argument which stands contrary to the knowledge of God, then we become weapons of destruction in the body of Christ and protectors of a stronghold of the enemy. To this, Paul says in 2 Corinthians chapter 10 verses 2 to 5,

> "Some people think that we live by the standards of the world. But though we live in the world, we do not wage war as the world does. The weapons we fight with are not the weapons of the world. On the contrary they have divine power to demolish strong holds. We demolish arguments and every pretension that sets itself up against the knowledge of God and we take captive every thought to make it obedient to Christ."

Divine Spiritual weapons wage war against the childish, argumentative pretensions, which can be the drive of our tongue, our emotional revelation, our pouting right to air our knowledge.

In Hebrews chapter 6 verse 4, after we are encouraged to give up our childish ways, the consequences of our refusal are evident. Verses 4 to 6 show us that those who fall away from the goodness of God are, "crucifying the Son of God all over again and subjecting him to public disgrace."

Disunity and childish quarrelling demonstrate our infancy. The Holy Spirit's working of the power and love of God is not demonstrated in gifts alone but in the growing maturity of God's people. Paul points out that our childish ways are rendered inactive, *katargeka*, by our adulthood. On this occasion *katargeo* is translated as "I put away" childish things. To be mature does not mean that childish things never occur again. We know that most men are at some time capable of them. Paul says that he puts them away. He exerts personal, mature, Holy Spirit restraint over the things which are contrary to the knowledge of God. He acknowledges that tongues can edify the individual (1 Corinthians 14 verse 4) and that he speaks in tongues more than anyone, according to verse 18, and is thankful to God for it. Paul's personal prayer life in tongues edifies him and builds him up in the spirit of God as he speaks to God and to his own spirit.

In 1 Corinthians 13 verse 11 Paul said, "when I was a child.... But when I became a man." A vital change has taken place. He has a different outlook. The, *logismos* of the child in stock taking every situation is the same as that in 2 Corinthians 10, which is taken down and brought captive to the obedience of Christ Jesus. It is the same logic which *keeps record* of wrong. It carries a logic of justice which says I will pay you back. It records what humanly is fair, especially for its own sake if it feels to be treated unfairly. The mature Christian does not, in love, keep a record for such competitive, so-called ministry.

At school, children say, "I'll get you at playtime." They show off how clever they are and one only needs to see children playing football to see how selfish they can be; a swarm of small bodies kicking wildly at whatever is before them. The ball shoots out from the pack and the swarm follows it, usually leaving one small body laid on the ground crying and holding a hurt leg. The chances are that he was kicked by a member of his own team eager to get the ball from anyone who had it. Occasionally the ball is with a winger and somewhere in the centre is someone in a striking position screaming at the top of his voice, "To me, to me!" The person in that striking position may also be the full back, who has wandered down the pitch to talk to the goalkeeper for the other side. The winger at this point has a choice to make. He knows that the one in the striking position should not be there. He should be a full back because he's not very good and was the last person left when they were picking the team. They didn't really want him but the teacher just pointed to him: "Right Percy, you are on their team." Now, will the winger pass? He pauses. If he passes, Percy will mess it up. Besides, if he can get there, he could score and be a hero. Too late! The swarm descends and the ball flies out again. Another body rolls in pain on the grass. The cries of "Foul ref!" are ignored. A couple of players look appealingly at the referee, pointing at the heap of injured footballer, but the game keeps going. So the appellants run to join the swarm.

This is childhood. Paul asks for adulthood. The mature may possess individual skill but they can be flattened when the swarm descends. Paul is looking for a team, a unit, a body. With real love we can do that which is so hard for infants to learn and yet is the most progressive skill: passing the ball. Selfishly keeping hold will most often cause us to miss the goal. Make love your goal.

We find in Romans 12 verse 9, that after Paul has spoken to a group of Christians about spiritual gifts, and about how we ought to allow ministries of gifts in the local Church, he goes on to speak about how gifts ought to operate in mature love.

> "Love must be sincere, unassuming and without hypocrisy, shrinking from evil, but cleaving to what is good. Taking the positive lead in making active steps to give preference to another with warm affectionate love. Do this with a burning passionate zeal, which never lets up. Strive for it, promote it, earnestly desire it amongst the brethren, never for a moment let the fire lower from

white heat in pursuit of it, this is your service to the Lord. Let the joy of the Lord which is the very strength of your salvation, characterise your every action to demonstrate where your hope really lies. If you are afflicted, endure with patience knowing that the death of human strife even against affliction, promotes the life of the Holy Spirit in you. Continue to steadfastly seek and find that deeper place of prayer, discovering the things of eternity, that they might by faith be brought into being on the earth. Be open hearted and open handed to those who are poor, believing that God who is no man's debtor will provide for your every need, and if someone persecutes you, or curses you then bless them, because when men curse you, Jesus counteracts the curse with blessing."

Some of this may sound impossible, but at the end of asking many such things of His disciples in His sermon on the mount, Jesus finishes with these words in Matthew 5 verse 48, "Be perfect, (*teleioi*) therefore, as your heavenly Father is perfect (*teleios*)."

Paul says, "I was a child, therefore I spoke and thought and reasoned like a child." When we were children our every unreasonable action made perfect sense to us at the time. Growing up requires training, learning, understanding, and sometimes discipline in order that our lives be shaped for mature adulthood. We have to be shaped spiritually to grow spiritually and quite often it takes a long time for God to form in us a different relationship which is not selfish or childish. If I asked, "Are you childish?" you would probably answer, "No of course not!" Or maybe you would come up with one of those Christian answers which we learn so well that it falls off the tongue, but has never changed our life. The truth is that I reason like a child. I don't think that I do, but then I wouldn't, because I think like a child. What my life needs is the pure, wise sacrificial love of God which is not selfish, but is able to lay down its life.

Paul's words also speak to us about personal responsibility for ensuring our own growth. Have you ever heard someone speaking of the fellowship to which they belong saying, "We speak in tongues in our church," or "We have a prophetic ministry in our fellowship?" When Paul says, "I was a child," he speaks of his own personal life and his own personal responsibility. The fact that we are part of the body gives to us a corporate love and accountability, but we still have the need for individual growth.

We come into God's kingdom at different times, each with different needs which are met in our personal relationship with the Lord, which is why Paul tells us that it is God who gives growth. We must, if we are to grow, be developing in personal relationship with Jesus, and learning his will. We cannot presume that because we are in a good fellowship that we are growing automatically. Nor can we believe that because in our opinion, our fellowship might be lacking, that we have therefore a reasonable excuse to stay as we are. Take the positive first step towards maturity. Seek personally the higher and more excellent way and become mature. Parts of the body don't mature in the same way or at the same time. Eyes come immediately, but teeth come later and have to change along the way. Take the first step of loving. If it is genuine then you will continue when it's difficult. Don't learn by your mistakes. When you do get it wrong, apologise, repent, go to the Lord and let Him be your teacher. Commend those who love and if they respond by saying, "Praise the Lord," then let the Lord be praised but be sure that while God takes the Glory, they take the encouragement.

In 1 Corinthians 14 verse 20, Paul, still seeking a loving ordered fellowship, uses these words,

"Brothers stop thinking like children. In regard to evil be infants, but in your thinking be perfect (*teleioi*) mature, fully grown, adult, men." We are to give up childish ways. Giving up is our repentant responsibility before God. It is not sufficient for a Church member of thirty years standing, to claim maturity on that basis alone. Many deacon and key worker positions in Churches are filled by people who were given office because they were there for such a long time. Such offices are not long service medals, for older may not mean wiser, except in the world's wisdom. Wiser, in 1 Corinthians chapter 2, is maturity which has the mind of Christ.

Therefore, as we aim for maturity, we have a responsibility to allow God to transform and renew our minds so that we can put aside childish ways and develop our personal relationship with Jesus. In mature love, we can, as God does, show favour to the less mature, less honourable parts of the church body so that we can all move forward together, towards that perfection of love and unity.

Chapter 9

When the perfect comes . . .

So what then is this state called perfection?

Perhaps an outline answer would be that it is
the state which the Almighty God, by the
working of the power of His love, calls us to aim
for, by being sanctified by every working of His
Holy Spirit, in the Church of the Lord Jesus
Christ.

It is the same state which Jesus encouraged in
His disciples when he told them to be perfect as
their heavenly Father is perfect (Matthew
chapter 5 verse 48). Clearly He is not speaking
of something which can only happen on
resurrection morning. In His sermon, Jesus has

just told the people of the way of love and how to live in it. The culmination is "Be perfect," something which is quite obviously attainable on earth.

In Hebrews chapter 10 verse 1 the writer says that the law is only a shadow of what is coming, not reality itself. This is why the offering of sacrifices year after year can never make anybody perfect. Then (verse 7) Jesus came with this declaration, "I am here to do your will O Lord." At verse 10, "By that will we have been made holy, through the sacrifice of Jesus made once for all." Verse 14: "Because by one sacrifice He has made perfect continually those who are being sanctified." If we are being sanctified, putting off the old for the sake of the new, then God continually regards us as perfect, so long as the process is taking place. Hebrews chapter 10 verse 14 says that Jesus' sacrifice gives us the opportunity to be continually made perfect. Even though God recognises my human imperfections, He will call me perfect while I am prepared to draw near to be forgiven.

If I trust myself or my own sacrifice then I am deemed to be unsanctified, trusting in the law that is a just shadow of what Jesus brought. However, if by faith I receive the grace of God then I am deemed to be perfect. He therefore calls me both perfect and being perfected.

Verse 16 of Hebrews chapter 10 tells us that the covenant which He has made is that He will put His laws in our hearts and write them on our minds, and he will remember our sins and lawless acts no more. This amazing truth is sometimes difficult for us to grasp because our view of perfection is not the same as the one of which the Bible speaks. To believe that we could ever really be like Jesus seems to denigrate Him and over-exalt ourselves. It somehow seems wrong even to think it because we are so aware of our own sin. But God knows about this already and has made sacrifice to atone for our sin through Jesus, His Son. We must accept that we can't make ourselves better; only He can do this work. The law which God now recognises is that of His own love perfected in Jesus. We cannot any longer break this law, since it represents a covenant made between the Father and the Son. If we fall upon this law it breaks us, and if it falls upon us we are smashed to pieces. It has become the very foundation and capstone of the building of the household of our faith.

Where we must begin is where we continue and where we end: cast upon this foundation, broken in repentance upon His love, continuing in that love until we touch its highest which is love, from faith to faith, from glory to ever increasing glory. In Hebrews chapter 12 verse 22, we are told that in coming to Jesus,

> "We have come to Mount Zion, to the heavenly Jerusalem, the city of the living God. We have come to thousands upon thousands of angels in joyful assembly and to the Church of the firstborn whose names are written in heaven. You have come to God, the Judge of all men, to the spirits of righteous men made perfect, to Jesus the mediator of a new covenant."

The pure heart of a righteous man is God's perfection.

Concerning our imperfect humanity, Paul, in Romans 7 verses 14 to 25, recognises that there are forces at work within our body of flesh. He refers to it as the body of death. He says that in his fleshly body there is a war going on. "Who will rescue me from this body of death?" he asks. "Thanks be to God who gives us the victory through our Lord Jesus Christ." There is a war going on in the members of the fleshly body, but in the spiritual body of Jesus where we dwell, perfection is the love of God which fills His temple (the body) and strife is at an end. Paul continues in all of his counsel to the churches to exhort us to no longer walk according to the flesh, but rather according to the Spirit. He continues in Romans 8 to describe the state in which we now live, delivered from the power of the flesh life.

> "There is now therefore no condemnation for those who are in Christ Jesus, for the law of the Spirit of life, (our foundation and capstone, where we now dwell), has set us free from the law of sin and death. For what the law was powerless to do in that it was weakened by our sinful nature, God did, by sending His own Son in the likeness of sinful man to be a sin offering."

God trusts His Son to be the originator and perfecter of faith.

In the law is an inherent weakness – the sin of man – which needed to be dealt with. God therefore deals with our sin through the cross and now we must continue to be partakers of the divine nature, and in our Spirit man and in our flesh, be formed into the character of Him who has become and is becoming our life. Just a little later in Romans 8 verse 5 and following, Paul speaks about a mind controlled by the Spirit being life and peace. When we die, we have a sure hope that we will be delivered from our fleshly bodies through bodily resurrection. For this time however, the victory over death is made real by the Holy Spirit at work, defeating the works of death and bringing life to our mortal flesh – winning the battle, so that we can experience resurrection power at work in our lives while we still live on this earth.

Horatio Toplady wrote the old hymn, "Rock of ages cleft for me, let me hide myself in Thee. Let the water and the blood, from Thy riven side which flowed, be of sin the double cure, cleanse me from its guilt and power." The power of the Blood, declares me guiltless of sin, and the sanctifying water of the Spirit cleanses me from its power by the ongoing revelation of Jesus in the mind.

When I was a young Christian, I was very conscious of sin in my life at many different levels. I was told by my mentors that I needed to feel sorry for my sin. I spent a lot of time trying to feel sorrier than I did, but feeling sorry continued to focus my gaze on the problem and not God's answer. True repentance is much more than sorrow. The contrite heart turns, not to the darkness of distress, but to the brightness of the Glory where forgiveness is found and where we are again encouraged to walk humbly before the Lord. 1 John chapter 1 verses 5 to 7 encourages us to walk in the light and live by the truth, not our human sorrow. If we walk in the light we have fellowship with one another and the blood of Jesus cleanses us from sin. We move closer, not away from the Lord. It is true that sin will drive us away. Don't be driven by sin.

In Philippians chapter 3, Paul again speaks of this life in the Spirit, this moving towards perfection. In verse 4 he says that he has every reason to be confident in his flesh, as he recites his huge list of worldly qualifications. However, at verse 7 he declares that whatever was to his profit, he now considers loss, even damaging for the sake of knowing Christ. His intellect, his theology, his middle class status, did not contribute except to the vileness of his sinful flesh life which he had to be rid of. Our translation of what Paul calls his worldly accomplishments is rather polite, but suffice to say he excreted them from his body and buried the stench in order to gain Christ and to be found in Him. This is the thing of surpassing greatness: having a righteousness which comes, not from the law or from our own achievements and strife, but freely, from faith in Christ. Paul continues with these remarkable words,

"I want to know Christ and the power of His resurrection and the fellowship of sharing in His sufferings, becoming like Him in His death, and so somehow attain to the resurrection from the dead."

Did he not yet know Christ? Did he not already have resurrection life? Yes! And Amen! But he had to continue in the life, through which God called him heavenward. He wasn't afraid of losing his salvation, but he was so gripped by it that this salvation had to be fully worked out. He had to work out what God was working in.

As he says in verse 12, Paul knows that he has not already achieved his aim, or been made perfect (*teleioo*) but he declares that he is determined to "press on to grasp that for which I in Christ have already been grasped." Grasped by Jesus, in order that in his mortal life he may take hold of this perfection, this maturity. "I strain towards it," he says. Then at verse 15, this strange remark:

"All of us who are perfect (*teleioo*) should have such a view of things, and if on some point you think differently, God will make it clear, only let us live up to what we have already attained."

If we profess to be spiritual then we cannot live by an assumption based on just one single experience. We must understand that the life which we have been given causes us, by faith, to grip it, to move closer to it and to fully embrace it. Because, as a child, I have it by right, I must now learn to grasp it in its full Holy Ghost reality. If I don't grasp it, I don't have it. The reality of our having salvation is that we are dynamically taking hold of it.

Galatians 5 verses 24 to 25 tells us that:

163

"Those who belong to Christ Jesus have crucified the sinful nature with its passions and desires. Since then we live by the Spirit, let us keep step with the Spirit."

I may find myself often out of step, but if I am honestly seeking to be in step, and desiring in my heart to please God and to love Him, and serve Him in His kingdom, then I am working out my salvation. The perfection for which God, through Christ, has grasped me, is being grasped by me.

In Philippians 3 verse 14, Paul refers to us being drawn heavenward with Jesus ahead of us allowing us to catch up, then moving on again, leading us heavenward. This is not just a journey towards death, but our spiritual development of Christ-like character, where the recognition of an area of sin causes us to have dealings with God and be cleansed, or where an opportunity to live by faith presents itself, or where love and humility in the body of Christ requires that we step back, allowing another to minister in order that they too might grow up in the gift. These are not just incidental occurrences, or momentary doings. These are to establish us in the place where we ought to be in Christ, nearer to Him, nearer to our heavenly calling than we were yesterday. That is why in verse 16 Paul says, "Therefore let us live up to what we have already attained."

The congregation with which I worship meets in a building which was named by those who originated that trust. It is called Ebenezer, an old fashioned name which causes people more readily to think of Scrooge rather than of God. Yet the name was given to a pile of stones in 1 Samuel chapter 7 verse12, with the words, "Hitherto the Lord has helped us." Ebenezer means 'stone of help'. Built between Mizpeh and Shen, it was the place where Israel, if they ever arrived back there, knew that they need not go back any further, because when they had arrived at this place on their inward journey, they knew the Lord was with them and their path was secure. In Genesis 31 verse 49, Laban and Jacob built a pile of stones at Mizpeh, which means 'watchtower'. There the Lord watched between the two of them that they did not deceive each other. Shen, from the root, 'shanan', means a place of a sharp point of diligent learning.

In our own lives we can build our Ebenezers at the places of our learning so that we need never go back to an old futile understanding. Having once learned the ways of the Lord, if we lose our way a little we can return, like a hiker on a foggy mountain, to the last cairn of our true understanding of the Lord's heart and direction for us. We can build it near to the place where the Lord watched between us and the brethren, at the place where last we were in the way of love. If we have taken a wrong course, we needn't in despair give up all hope of finding a way of restoration, but we can fix our gaze on Him who is the way and begin again to walk in fellowship. We don't have to go down a snake back to square one. We can know that hitherto the Lord is with me, and continue to live up to what we have already attained.

It is important then that we keep short accounts and seek to live the life of the Spirit, not falling back, but keeping step with the Holy Ghost. In Matthew chapter 19 verse 21, Jesus is speaking with the rich young ruler, who thus far had kept the law and yet was lacking something. Jesus said,

> "If you want to be perfect, (*teleios*) then go, sell what you have and give to the poor. And you will have treasure in heaven, then come and follow me."

He wasn't able to give and therefore he wasn't able to follow the Lord heavenward. He went away very sad. Where Jesus calls, then we must follow. This is not just through answering an altar call, but by living according to the dynamic, onward call of Jesus, towards that which He calls perfection.

Again in John chapter 17 verse 23, Jesus is in prayer for the Church. He prays that we (as the NIV translation records it) may be in complete unity. The Greek phase here is, *teteleiomenoi eis en*, meaning 'having been perfected in one'. Here we see perfection in unity being possible between brethren, even as Jesus is perfectly one with the Father. How can this perfection be? The preceding verse gives us the answer: "I have given them the glory that you gave me, that they may be one as we are one."

Verse 14 tells us that we are not of this world any more than Jesus is. In love our heavenly Father has called us to be His children; a new family, a new household and a new kingdom. If we look at verse 18 we see that just as the Father sent Jesus into the world, so He sends us. Whilst I do not disagree with the interpretation of most that to be sent like Jesus means to be sent out full of power, the primary meaning in its context has to be that we don't belong to the world any more as we were taken out, and therefore we have to be sent back in. We were lifted from its grip, its control and its power. We now have a new life in the Spirit and have lost our membership, our citizenship of the world and have become citizens of the Kingdom of God. As children of God we are members of the body of Christ and just as Jesus had to be sent from God, so also must we.

Jesus, the perfect Son of God, was born sinless, and yet during His life on earth, according to Hebrews chapter 5 verse 7 to 9,

"He offered up prayers and petitions with loud cries, to the one who could save Him from death, and He was heard because of His reverent submission. Although He was a Son, He learned obedience from what He suffered and once made **perfect** He became the source of eternal salvation for those who obey Him."

We too, as sons of the true and living God, have been made clean and being perfectly joined, baptised by the Holy Spirit into Jesus Christ, must now learn to live in reverent submission to the one who can save us from death and give to us that resurrection, which Jesus has and Paul strives to attain. Even though we are sons, it is in our submission that we are made perfect.

171

According to John chapter 17 verse 19, in Christ we are truly sanctified, and therefore, according to Hebrews chapter 10 verse 14, we are made perfect: ". . . by one sacrifice he has made perfect forever those who are being made holy."

In John chapter 17 verse 22, Jesus confirms that we are given the, "ever increasing glory of God", which was firstly given to Him. If we begin to walk according to the Spirit in obedience to Jesus, then the life of the Spirit which we manifest is the character of Jesus, not only gifts of power. We are not dependent on ourselves for perfection in unity, nor for being made perfect in love, but we are responsible for continuing to walk in the new and perfect nature which has been given to us that this nature might mature.

Most Christians readily accept that we are forgiven all of our sins. So then when in our lives, which are being brought into submission to the living God in gift ministry, service and unity, might we be regarded as perfect, mature, whole, trustworthy adults in the love of God? Is it possible in our mortal lives that we can grow until we attain to the full measure of perfection found in Jesus? Ephesians chapter 4 verse 13 says that we can "reach unity in the faith and in the knowledge of the Son of God and become mature, attaining to the whole measure of the fullness of Christ." In his letter to the Colossian Church, Paul writes,

"We proclaim Him, counselling and teaching everyone with all wisdom so that we may present everyone 'perfect' in Christ. To this end I labour, struggling with all the energy He so powerfully works in me. I want you to know how strenuously I am exerting myself," (chapter 1 verse 28).

Here he describes what this perfection looks like:

"My purpose is that they may be encouraged in heart and united in love, so that they might have a complete understanding, in order that they might know the mystery of God, namely Christ, in whom are hidden all the treasures of wisdom and knowledge."

Unity in love in which we have full knowledge and wisdom in Christ is our perfection. Later in Colossians chapter 4 verse 12, we find Epaphras praying that we might, "Stand firm in the will of God, perfect, (*teleioi*) and fully assured."

Let us now look again at James who speaks of "The perfect gifts" in chapter 1 verse 17, "perfect law", chapter 1 verse 25 and "perfect man", chapter 3 verse 2. The things which God creates have no fault. They are always perfect, always complete and fit for His purpose. His love gift of Jesus, His gift of salvation and His grace gifts are all perfect. His law of love in Jesus, which He upholds and which cannot be broken, is perfect. His regenerate man, completely forgiven, already made perfect and yet still being made perfect in the death of the flesh life, is not just looking forward to the resurrection, but already being made alive by the Spirit which raised Jesus from the dead. Our foretaste of eternity is the death and Holy Spirit resurrection life at work now in our mortal flesh.

Finally, when the perfect comes, that which is in part, (*ek merous*) will be rendered powerless. If the body, not the gift, is from various parts and only a part of the whole, and immature, then the body, not the gift is being perfected, this being the aim to which the whole of the New Testament points. It is the body, the church, that is not yet perfect, not the gift. If I receive a part of a car, an engine for instance, and I am told that the whole is on the way, then I would expect that one day, even if I have to build it myself, I will eventually have a complete car. If that which is imperfect is replaced by the perfect, then it will be a perfect body which replaces the imperfect body, and if the imperfection is a result of the body being fragmented, then that body will be united. Could it be that Jesus is looking for a body which is not fragmented, not infantile and not immature but mature and joined in love which is the bond of perfection? Is this the perfection of which Paul speaks? Not the discord, but the building which will survive to eternity even through the fire of God. This perfection is that which is only possible by the love which comes from the throne of God and without which every gift and action is nothing. This perfection is members of the Church of Jesus reaching maturity, having learned the way of love, and holding back a tongue or a prophecy in order that others might be that manifestation of the Holy Spirit which causes growth

Chapter 10

Now we see but a poor reflection but then face to face . .

Some believe that the time when we no longer see a poor reflection must obviously mean when Jesus comes again since that is when we will see Him face to face. I believe that the gifts of the Holy Spirit will remain but I do not believe that 1 Corinthians 13 verse 12 is referring to Jesus' return. Paul speaks about a reflection on another occasion in 2 Corinthians chapter 3 verse 18. He is speaking about the glorious ministry of the Holy Spirit, when the dull veil of the law is removed from our mind; when through the revelation of Jesus, in whose face we see God, we are being transformed into His likeness with ever increasing glory which comes from the Lord, who is the Spirit. He is speaking of the time when the Church, His body, becomes the glorious reality of the life of Jesus, in all His love, His power, His Holy Spirit giftings, signs and wonders, reflecting clearly the Jesus whose Holy Spirit is fully at work in His body. At that time, the Church at Corinth, like so many of the fellowships of believers today, was an extremely poor reflection, compared to that perfection towards which the Holy Spirit was directing them. The Lord, who is the Spirit, requires that the veil of our consciousness, our mind, is removed in order that we see Him face to face.

Luke chapter 6 verse 40 tells us that no student is greater than His master, but when he is fully trained he will be like His master. In our life changing relationship with Jesus, we should become less of self and more of Him. Of course if I asked has anyone seen God, you would no doubt come to the conclusion that, "No man has seen the Father, except the Son, who is at the Father's side and He has made Him known." In John chapter 14 verse 9, when Philip asks that Jesus show him the Father, Jesus replied, "Anyone who has seen me has seen the Father." "Don't you believe that I am in the Father and the Father in me?" "It is the Father living in me who is doing the work." Later, in verse 20, Jesus goes on to say, "On that day you will realise that I am in my Father and you are in me." The day in question is when Jesus goes to the Father and his disciples will begin to do the greater works which Jesus spoke of. "And I will show myself to him." The glory of Jesus, who is in the Father, is visible in His Church as we are transformed. We can see Him: "I will show myself to you."

Philip sees the Father in Jesus because He and the Father are one; He is in the Father. The world sees Jesus in the Church when we are in Him and perfected in His love.

In 2 Corinthians chapter 4 verse 6, Paul tells us that God has made His light shine in our hearts to give us the light of the knowledge of the Glory of God in the face of Christ. We need to seek His face. We are so easily distracted to seek His hand. The gift is from His hand, but the Glory is in the unveiled face of Jesus, clearly visible in His body as we are being perfected in love. We are not to be a poor reflection, but with open face, truthful speech in love, gifts and signs constrained by the love of God and with decency and order in worship for the sake of others but our own absolute abandonment to the Lord, we are to become a revelation of Jesus

Christ who so richly lives in those who by faith have believed Him and received the Holy Spirit. Not a mere reflection but a light shining in the darkness. Now we see but a poor reflection. When the perfect comes, we will see face to face.

Conclusion

I cannot find a single reference to the full canon of scripture being a time of cessation and those who believe this and purport by its proclamation to elevate scripture do no such thing. Since the Bible does not say such a thing it can only be said that the cessationist view is based on experience, or lack of it, which drives to a conclusion contrary to what the Bible says. It is sadly the style of many cessationists to present a catalogue of the bizarre as fodder for their argument. This of course is no argument, since the actions of either the few or the many do not disestablish the truth. The convolution of the argument around Biblical texts which have no bearing on this matter equally does little to persuade the reader of the validity of any argument. To seek to make unreasonable comparisons of an Old Testament prophet with those prophesies in the New Testament Church which Paul clearly acknowledges and validates, does not create an argument of any substance. We live in a world where truth is no longer regarded as absolute, but whether the world or the Church believe it, what God has said will not change. Rather it is necessary for us to change and be discovered by the truth.

Gifts will remain until Jesus comes again, and the whole work of God in the Holy Spirit will never fail or fall. It remains important for us to discover not only where we can demonstrate the Holy Spirit's power, although we often lack because of our faith, but also when we can better serve in the building, by encouraging others to take the more honourable place, while we withhold our gift. This is a higher calling and honour, both of the body and of the Lord. If Paul's plea is to be heard then we must also learn different disciplines in the Church. Tongues and their abuse ought to be challenged. Prophecies should be weighed and if necessary corrected by the mature. Knowledge should be properly sought and imparted in an honest and righteous way. 1 Corinthians 14 speaks again of these three issues and says that these in particular are areas where we can, for the sake of order, remain silent. God is a God of miracle and He has not ceased so to be. It is wrong to give to Him public dishonour by our disorder.

1 Corinthians 13 is not an explanation of gifts remaining until Jesus comes. Of course until He does come, the Church will continue to be built by the Spirit of God at work in those gifts which lift us from our infancy to maturity – to

perfection. Jesus has said that against this building, even the gates of Hell will not prevail.

Printed in the United Kingdom
by Lightning Source UK Ltd.
133917UK00002B/1/P